PRAISE FOR FAY JAC
REHOBOTH BEACH DIARIES

"Her columns . . . are laugh out loud funny and the best part is that Jacobs is sincere . . . Those who enjoyed Jacobs' (other collections) will not be disappointed and those reading her for the first time will understand why she's such a beloved columnist."
—Jane van Ingen, *Lambda Book Report*

"It's an intelligent, hysterically funny and occasionally poignant look at how we live today, with hopes for tomorrow. Recommended for everyone, male or female, gay or straight. Five stars out of five." —*Echo Magazine*

"She makes you laugh and she makes you think—and then you laugh again, and again and again."
—Comic Jennie McNulty

"Every bit as sardonic, witty, sarcastic and insightful as her other books!"
—Richard LaBonte, *San Francisco Bay Times*

"Fay Jacobs' hilarious dispatches are funny, touching—and real. This is a true laugh riot, as Fay wittily takes on sexuality, politics, relationships, and day-to-day dilemmas." —*Insight Out Book Club*

"Every tale is masterfully told—these memorable memoirs . . . are both pleasure and treasure."
—Anna Furtado, *JustAboutWrite*

"Fay Jacobs' sharp wit turns frustrating everyday events into laugh-out-loud medicine worthy of award-winning stand-up comedy. My sides hurt long after reading, but I still beg for more. Keep writing!" —author Carsen Taite

"Fay's writing is everything we've come to expect—humorous, insightful, and savvy. Fay finds universal messages in everyday experiences, entertaining while reminding us of all that binds us together. Laugh, cry, and above all, rejoice with Fay Jacobs' newest collection!"

—Radclyffe, author of Trauma Alert

"Pure Borscht Belt gold—a funny, wisely observed and politically astute read."—*Out in Print*

Fay Jacobs' Rehoboth Beach Diaries:

As I Lay Frying
Fried & True
For Frying Out Loud
Time Fries

For Amber: Enjoy! Laugh a lot! Fay Jacobs

FRIED & CONVICTED
REHOBOTH BEACH UNCORKED

FAY JACOBS

Bywater BOOKS

Ann Arbor
2017

Bywater Books

Bywater Books First Edition: April 2017

Cover designer: TreeHouse Studio

Cartoon on page 217 courtesy of Rob Waters

Bywater Books
PO Box 3671
Ann Arbor MI 48106-3671
www.bywaterbooks.com

ISBN: 978-1-61294-093-9 (print)
ISBN: 978-1-61294-094-6 (ebook)

To my wife Bonnie and the Usual Subjects

Table of Contents

2016

Foreword

Fay Jacobs and I have been through a lot together over the past two decades. I've written introductions to four of her essay collections, and I couldn't be happier to write the fifth.

Fried & Convicted was written over the last few years, and it chronicles the joy of gaining equal marriage rights for same-sex couples, tales of Icelandic lagoons, Provincetown adventures and words about lesbians of a certain age. And it tells a few harrowing personal stories, such as Bonnie's unnerving medical diagnosis, the time Fay went kayaking with alligators, or came up with a public relations scheme to rescue my beloved dog after she was stolen from my house. I'll say that again: MY DOG WAS STOLEN FROM MY HOUSE.

But this isn't about me (but seriously, someone stole my dog; you can read about it in "The Case of the Purloined Pooch" in this book). This is about a woman who truly lives out loud, and this past year, she's taken that adage literally. Fay and I have many shared experiences in the theater. Except that for most of our two decades of friendship, I was the one onstage, and Fay was seated firmly in the director's chair. She's still in that chair, but now that chair is on stage. She's embarked on a new career as a "sit-down comic," reading her essays to crowds on land and sea.

She begins her show with an adage she long ago learned from her father Mort, who always said "Nothing is so terrible if you get a good story to tell." Those are words that Fay lives by, and we're all the better for it.

I got my dog back. Fay was not eaten by alligators. Bonnie got well. There are some great stories here. And nothing is so terrible. Enjoy!

—Eric C. Peterson
Rehoboth Beach, Delaware

Prologue

Here we go again! This writer is still aging gracelessly in Rehoboth Beach, Delaware.

In the two decades my wife Bonnie and I have lived at the beach, we've resided in one boat, two condos, two houses, and an RV; we've shared our homes with a succession of schnauzers, and been domestic-partnered, civil-unioned and married, twice, through a variety of paperwork and ceremonies.

I love my wife, my life in Rehoboth, and having the privilege of writing about any topic that catches my fancy. I continue to have a blast as a columnist, despite having reached and surpassed retirement age.

As of 2015, I've become a performer as well, touring with my one-woman show *Aging Gracelessly: 50 Shades of Fay.* Who knew I could break into show business at an age when I'd be more likely to break a hip?

And one single principle has guided me along this sometimes bumpy but always interesting road.

My father always said: Nothing is ever so horrible if you wind up with a good story to tell. And have I got stories. Some are fun, some are distressing, and a lot of them are absolutely infuriating. But they've all been fodder for the storyteller in me.

And frankly, this legacy about taking lemons and turning them into typewritten lemonade was the best advice my father ever gave me—especially since the rest from that era tended toward "It wouldn't kill you to wear a dress to your sister's wedding" and "You'll never find a husband if you buy a house with another girl." Although he was right on both counts.

Along with my almost 40 years of watching, participating in, and writing about our LGBT march toward full civil rights, I've taken time to have a hell of a lot of fun, and written those stories, too.

And following my dad's advice, I try to find something worthwhile to take from just about every stupid, annoying, or awful thing that happens.

So here comes my fifth collection of essays, these particular ones having been published in the magazines *Letters from CAMP Rehoboth* and *Delaware Beach Life*. I have also included a keynote speech I had the privilege to be invited to give at the Golden Crown Literary Society Conference in July 2016. I love the topic of passing along our culture—and I am happy to share my take on it with you.

So here come the stories. And the opinions. Duck and cover, my friends. I'm letting the ink fly.

January 2014

I must come clean about my addiction. I am a streaming junkie.

Streaming. It sounds like something out of a tree-hugger nature magazine. But no, it's technology. I'm sure I'm light-years behind the curve on this, but somehow I stumbled into a Blu-ray DVD player and Netflix. There it was, the world of video streaming before my bulging eyeballs.

Oh, it was casual use at first. We clicked Netflix and watched a movie or two on demand. Then, over a period of weeks, we watched the Netflix series *Orange Is the New Black*, marveling at our ability to watch two episodes a night if we so chose. What a great new technology! Freedom from network schedules!

Then it happened. One cold January weekend we found ABC's *Scandal* and watched the 2011 premier episode. And right after the credits, without any further action on our part, the TV counted down 30 seconds until the next episode started. My spouse and I exchanged furtive glances. Should we? It was already 10:30 p.m. What the heck.

Then it was 11:15, with 10, 9, 8, 7 . . . third episode on deck.

Now if you've never seen this show and you might watch it one day, stop here. Spoiler Alert. But if you've already ogled three years of this crazy political potboiler, you will know exactly how we got hooked.

That first night, we dragged ourselves away from the TV after episode four, which featured wicked political scandals, murders, spin doctoring and steamy love affairs. But by 8 a.m. we were back at the boob tube, drinking our steaming coffee, glued to our streaming TV, following the wild goings-on in the Oval Office. I hadn't been planted in front of the TV like this on a Saturday morning since I was in diapers watching Daffy Duck.

At this point, diapers might have helped, as we hardly made time to visit the powder room. "Do you want lunch?" my mate asked. Lunchtime already? We hit pause, slapped together peanut butter and jelly sandwiches and resumed our stream of unconsciousness. "The president's been shot! Oh no, how will Olivia spin this? Will the Chief of Staff allow his husband to adopt a baby?"

Scandal streamed into our home for hours on end, like an exciting, edgy, steamy, raw political bodice ripper. I was thoroughly, giddily, addicted.

How badly? By Saturday night we were well into season two and resentful that a friend's birthday would take us to a favorite restaurant for glorious food and Cosmopolitans. I'd rather stay home with a case of the streaming meemies? This was trouble.

So we changed horses in midstream and went to dinner. Even the Grey Goose couldn't keep me from needing my fix.

Rushing back from dinner, we dove into our living-room bunker and hunkered down for another streaming pile of *Scandal*, coming up only for air, popcorn, or the unavoidable potty break. Who really shot the president? Did the Supreme Court Justice die of natural causes? Who stole the voting machine card?

By Sunday, bleary-eyed and weakened from lack of exercise, we saw snowflakes start to fall. Woo-hoo!!!! A Monday snow day would mean *Scandal* streaming for hours on end. In the countdown between episodes we checked the weather channel and high-fived.

"Another episode will begin in 20 seconds ..."

We awoke Monday morning to six inches of new-fallen show and swollen eyes from our late night stream-a-thon. Grabbing Visine and bathrobes we headed right back to the stream of the crime.

Kidnappings, rekindled romance, spies, moles, press briefings, stunning clothes and ...

Sleeping, paying bills, even writing columns became mere irritants compared to the constant streaming of *Scandal*. If we ate and drank at all, it was hunched over the coffee table in front of the TV. Forget getting dressed, or doing the dishes, forget everything but finding out who did what dirty tricks to who on *Scandal*.

10 . . . 9 . . . 8 . . . 7 . . .

Plunging back into the intrigue, we lapped up another exciting forty-three minutes of top-notch television. That's when it happened. The video signal went kaflooey. The screen went to black. And when it came back on 30 seconds later, my television asked me for our Netflix name and password.

Excuse me? Password? How would I know? I signed up months ago. Do you know how many password decisions and changes I've made to my zillion password-protected accounts since then? Is it my book title? Mother's maiden name? First dog? High school boyfriend?

Hysterical, I fled to my computer, googled Netflix and clicked Forgot Password. They promised to send me a code on my cell phone. Cell phone? I hadn't seen it in days. A frantic search revealed nothing so I called myself from my house phone to find my cell phone, which rang from beneath the sofa cushions where it had become buried and forgotten during the scandalous binge.

Code in hand, I raced to the television to reset my Netflix password. The screen blinked Enter Password, over and over, taunting me. Enter Password!!!!!! Enter Password!!!!!!

Suddenly, I had an epiphany. I understood that my television set had just performed an intervention. It was sister, nephew, best friend all in one. Sure, I denied my addiction at first, but then I knew what I should do. I hollered "Uncle!"

I turned off the TV and made us a couple of cold turkey sandwiches. We entered streaming rehab. We got dressed. We went out. We ate a meal at a table.

I've been clean for months now. But there are days when I still wonder about the scandals I am missing as I lust for a really intense binge-watch. I can stream, can't I???

January 2014

Oh my. We've just come back from the trip of a lifetime. The words I have been assigned in this column cannot do it justice, but I will try.

In the midst of another freakin' winter snow storm in Baltimore, we flew out to Quito, Ecuador, on the flippin' equator. Nice improvement. And we took the requisite awkward photo with one foot in the Northern Hemisphere and the other in the Southern. Tourons, indeed.

From Quito we flew 600 miles to the island of Baltra in the Galapagos, traveled by bus the short distance to the coast, donned life jackets, and took a 16-person inflatable boat to our anchored ship. Our luxurious Celebrity cruise ship welcomed only 100 passengers. While this was no gay cruise, using our gaydar we immediately spied our 10 percent and had great company. Plus, we met several straight couples we came to adore, so the diversity was a blast.

Every day we left the ship by inflatable boat to go to a different island. The first day was probably the most fantastic since it was such a glorious surprise to be up close and personal with sea lions, iguanas, sea turtles, and a bevy of birds.

Since there are no island predators, certainly not humans, the animals have no fear. We were told to stay at least eight feet from the animals but if they chose to come closer, what could we do? At one point a friend stopped to sit under a tree to tie her shoe and a honking sea lion came up and used her butt for a pillow. Stranger things have happened, but not much.

These fabulous creatures lumbered up to us, snorted, scratched, and generally went about their business. We saw nursing sea lions, swimming sea turtles, and fish-swallowing pelicans, in what truly personified a Big Gulp. Penguins hopped around in pairs, cormorants dried their wings in the wind, and frigate birds swooped overhead like the Blue Angels.

Then there was the day of the iguana. Piles of them, actually, littering the beach, happily ignoring the camera-carrying, floppy-hatted tourist species. I became so addicted to snapping photos I begged Bonnie to stop me so I could actually look around and take it all in. Never had I seen such a magical environment.

One day we took a long walk along a portion of an island formed by a 1998 volcanic eruption. The lava and shale formations looked like stunning sculptures, modern art, and a stark, unforgiving landscape. Heaven and hell together, beautiful and forbidding at the same time.

One gay boy clucked his tongue at finding a two-foot square piece of shale that had broken off a formation. He picked it up and searched for where it came from. Sure enough, he found the exact spot and fit it back together like a jigsaw puzzle. "It was so messy!" he joked.

Darwin's theories of evolution and nature's uncanny ability to persevere were all around us. To see a tiny new-growth cactus peek out from a wall of inhospitable lava told the tale.

Later, we walked to Darwin's Lake, where flamingos stood on one foot, grazing from the reeds growing from underneath of the water. When the naturalists told us that the birds spend seven hours a day eating, everyone was astonished. I don't know why. We'd been doing just that on the ship.

When it came time for snorkeling I donned the big ugly wet suit and gave it a try. I was all right at first, floating, head down, gazing at the beautiful array of colorful fish. In my wonderment I didn't notice the current pushing me pretty far out, where I bumped a rock and scraped my knee. Gee, Bonnie was no longer nearby, and I panicked a little, glad to see one of our inflatables and its crew hovering not too far away.

They'd taught us a signal for requesting help—kind of a loop with my arm, over my head. The best I could do at that point was flail my arms, but the crew recognized that as the universal evacuation plea.

The boat came quickly and hauled me aboard. As the lone casualty of our 16-person tour, I felt humiliated—until I saw the others gasping for air, struggling back to shore, stumbling out of the water as if they'd made the Cuba to Key West swim. I began to feel less humiliated than clever.

Back aboard the mother ship, I unzipped my wet suit, surprised I didn't hear myself deflate like a beach ball with its valve open. I peeled off the rubber clothing and got immediately into a dry martini.

The naturalists warned us that we were not allowed to take any lava, shells, rocks, or sand off the islands and onto the ship. They didn't count the pounds of sand in our hair, not to mention our privates. And if they could think of a polite way to get that back, I suspect they would.

A main attraction was the Blue-footed Booby—a gull-like bird with bright blue webbed feet. According to the naturalists, the brighter the blue, the more attractive the bird is to the opposite sex. On the heels of that description we saw fornicating sea tortoises, with one female entertaining lots of different males, for sessions lasting up to eight hours. When done, the males continue to swim and the female drags herself, exhausted, up onto the shore. I would imagine so. Between the Boobies and the turtle antics it was like the "The Real Housewives of Galapagos."

My favorite island adventure happened on one of only two inhabited islands. The naturalists told us that the sea lions were the original island occupants, with the people arriving later. Ergo, people defer to the sea lions as natives.

We got off our boats at the pier, and spied benches for people waiting for the ferries and boats. The folks sitting on those benches were equally divided between human beings and sea lions. There was a park in the town, built for the human inhabitants' children, but it was currently being used by sea lions. Do you know that playground equipment with bright-colored tubes where kids can slide into sandboxes or water? The sea lions were using it. And appearing to enjoy themselves. Honest.

We got back to our ship and an adorable sea lion was sitting on the swim platform welcoming us home. "Good thing we have stairs up to the higher floors," said our naturalist. "On other boats, with ramps, it's not unusual to come down to breakfast and find sea lions in the dining room!"

One of our last stops on the cruise was a sanctuary for giant tortoises, which looked like Volkswagens. Some of them were over 100 years old. We were told it takes a giant tortoise two to three weeks to digest a meal, which I related to because that pretty much happens to me if I go to Burger King.

At the sanctuary we heard about Lonesome George, a huge old tortoise who recently passed away. Apparently he was lousy in the dating department and the island was not incubating any tortoises. When the government of Ecuador borrowed a giant tortoise of the same species from the San Diego Zoo, voila! All of a sudden there were 1,200 baby tortoises. Our guides told us that Diego, as he was called, managed all that without a little blue pill.

Yup, Darwin had it right. Survival of the fittest. Those of us less fit survived too, as it was an adventure, but not too strenuous. We ate and drank our fill, took thousands of pictures and cannot recommend a trip to the Galapogos Islands highly enough.

And I came home with a T-shirt proclaiming "I Love Boobies!" Luckily, on the front of the shirt there's a drawing of the blue-footed kind.

February 2014

There are a lot of things that strike me as absurd these days.

Since we last spoke, we had the controversy over the Broadway show *Kinky Boots* in the Macy's Thanksgiving Day Parade. There was outrage because drag queens were to perform. Really? When it comes to Broadway, why aren't the complaining cretins upset by the child abuse dealt out by Miss Hannigan in *Annie* or Fagin teaching kids to steal in *Oliver?* And why is it okay to celebrate a murderer who slits throats and his sidekick who bakes the bodies into meat pies in *Sweeny Todd?* Seriously, all these particular drag queens do is save a straight man's shoe business. Puleeze. This warrants controversy?

And of course there was the brain trust from *Duck Dynasty.* When asked about LGBT issues, who didn't expect Mr. Duck to spout hateful bullpucky? Frankly, somebody looking as nasty and sounding as stupid as that guy shrieking against gays makes us look like angels. They should have avoided the backlash by keeping him on the air to continue to make a dumbo of himself.

And then there's the whole falling of dominoes in the marriage equality map. What's absurd is the hostile response over something that is now so inevitable. Save your energy, bigots; you lost this one. In a big way.

And I've been celebrating the whole marriage controversy. In fact, as that fabulous old queen Noel Coward sang in 1932, recently "I went to the most mahvelous party!"

It was the wedding of two young male friends and the event blew my mind in so many ways.

Frankly, since marriage equality swept Delaware, Maryland, and environs, I've been to a lot of weddings, including one of my own. And all of them have been the coupling of old poops like us, together for decades and finally permitted to make it legal. Not that the events haven't been gorgeous, with loving families, white tablecloths, and champagne toasts. They have. And it's been glorious.

But there's something special about attending a wedding where the two grooms are of the traditional young marriageable age, a wedding with all the pomp and circumstance of the big weddings we used to lust after. Or at least wish we had the legal right to emulate, if not the actual desire to go out in a hail of rice or birdseed as is now the environmentally friendly tradition.

Here was a wedding of two wonderful young men, with a gaggle of groomsmen assisting the groomsmaids with their makeup and rearranging the angles of their corsages. Turnabout certainly was fair play as one groomsman hastily re-hemmed a groomsmaid's dress. Another insisted I wear eyeliner and applied it to my droopy lids himself.

There was a Gayd of Honor, a wedding planner and a stage manager, a serenade by members of the Gay Men's Chorus of Washington prior to the ceremony, and a drag queen emcee at the reception. Yes, if it's worth doing, it's worth overdoing and this wedding was spectacular.

For me, this was a very special event. I had been asked by one of the grooms to be a stand-in for his mom, who would not attend. She missed an amazing chance to escort her handsome son and watch, with enormous pride, as he married his soul mate.

For his part, the soul mate invited his traditional Southern parents. They were in full attendance and did not blink once. Not when the marriage officiate pronounced them groom and groom and they kissed, not each time silverware tapped crystal at the reception and the grooms were required to kiss some more, and certainly not during their first dance to the iconic "Endless Love." Cheers to them.

Following the requisite professional picture-taking (I think it's safe to say that as the mother of the groom, I may have been the butchest one in the wedding party) we got the celebration going.

This reception was as different as it was the same. Unlike some straight weddings, here, when the DJ played "Dancing Queen" the song was never more appropriate. And to see the dance floor swamped by men with only a spattering of women in the crowd struck an unusual chord as well.

First came "The Electric Slide" led by a gaggle of guys, followed by "It's Raining Men," complete with synchronized choreography. The only time the dance floor emptied was for "YMCA," as if to say "That old thing!" to the number generally marking the only dance floor filler at many straight weddings.

The oft-played dance floor version of musical chairs became musical Cher's at this wedding, with the guests rushing for seats to Cher's recordings.

During the toasts, the straight best friend of one of the grooms provided some warm and wonderful words, while the other groom's best friend provided a moving, tear-inducing story.

And, since the wedding was held on Veterans Day, with one groom having served our country prior to "Don't Ask, Don't Tell" being lifted, the event was even more moving.

From the rhinestones affixed to seating cards to the cake-cutting antics, this was a traditional wedding. When the grooms left the reception by limo amid soap-bubble blowing well-wishers, this wedding was a shoo-in for the phrase, "the more things change the more they remain the same."

This wedding looked like 2013 America. And nothing that *Kinky Boots* haters or dirty duck callers can say can take away the glee.

March 2014

THE CASE OF THE PURLOINED POOCH

My granddog is the Toast of Washington, D.C. By the time her publicist is done, Margo the Cockapoo may be a national household name.

You might have heard the tale of the purloined pooch by now, which is what the *Washington Post* called Margo. Do I get publicity in the *Post*? No. My son's cockapoo does.

If you have not heard the horrible tale with the perfect outcome, here are the details. If you missed this freaky story, here it is in all its angst, agony, and absolutely heart-warming outcome.

It started when I took a phone call from my son Eric Peterson on a wintry Thursday night. He was agitated and hysterical. His Capitol Hill home had been broken into, all his electronics had been stolen, and his two-and-a-half-year-old dog Margo was gone, too. Not only was she gone, but since her leash, food, and toys were also gone, it was clear she was part of the looting operation. My granddog was stolen property.

I try to find humor everywhere, but there was nothing funny here. We were devastated. Bonnie and I got to D.C. as soon as possible to help with the hunt, but within ten minutes of being called, the D.C. police were already on the scene and the entire Gay Men's Chorus of Washington was on alert and pitching in to help their pal Eric get his best friend back.

In a social media frenzy, chorus members and friends posted Margo's photo, tweeted the news, and starting printing up MISSING posters and flyers.

As an old public relations flack I knew that if there was any chance at all of getting Margo back we had to get an enormous amount of publicity. And as only money talks, we knew we had to offer an impressive, if not ridiculously large, reward.

My financial manager almost stroked out when she heard the purpose of my $10,000 withdrawal, but Eric and I hoped that

15

number was big enough to get us on television with a plea for her return.

It was impressive enough. By noon Friday, WRC-TV and FOX5 were on the scene, interviewing Eric, filming the ransacked townhouse, lovingly photographing and talking about Margo's empty, overturned crate and her distraught human companions.

Meanwhile, Facebook and Twitter lit up with BRING MARGO HOME messages, starring Margo's BFF Cara and her humans, begging for her return. The reward was posted all over the place. The police set up a tip-line phone number.

Bonnie, Eric, and I spent the long, horrid afternoon attempting to keep busy with posters and tweets, reassuring ourselves that it was not like Margo had escaped and was running around in the cold on the dangerous streets. We suspected she was inside, warm, and being harbored by some stupid petty thief who cruelly and callously wanted somebody else's dog. It was not a pretty time.

Throughout the afternoon, a Capitol Hill dog-walking service, Saving Grace Pet Care (plug, plug!), posted REWARD posters all over town, while Facebook published pleas, pictures, and FIND MARGO posts.

By 5 p.m. news time, reports of the missing Margo were all over the tube, in heart-wrenching human and canine interest stories, emotionally and sensationally crafted by TV reporters and film editors. The dramatic film had Eric pleading for his companion's return, news anchors sensationally telling the tale, and photos of the missing pooch posted on camera.

"Man Desperate to Find Missing Dog!" (hell, Jewish grand-mothers desperate to find missing dog!) Tweet: #FINDMARGO. "Reward offered, no questions asked, for stolen canine!"

By Friday evening we left Eric with friends, who had instructions to provide enough Maker's Mark so the guy could get some shut-eye. We made the sad trip back to Reho and somehow got ourselves some sleep as well, but it wasn't easy.

My cell phone rang at 8 a.m. "I got her back! The police have her! I'm going down to the station to get her!!!!!!!"

Sometimes there's nothing you can say but the quintessential OMG.

Early in the morning a detective had called Eric and asked "What's the name of your dog?" Eric responded. When the officer called, "Margo! Margo!!" and the dog went ballistic, the detective said to Eric, "We've got your dog."

So Eric headed for the police station, alerting the TV reporters he'd spoken to along the way. After all, thousands of viewers should get the good news, too. And TV news people adore a two-part story with an incredibly happy ending.

It seems that the police tip line got a hit late Friday night. The tipster saw Margo being walked on the street not far from the scene of break-in. The person didn't know the Margo story, but told a friend about the guy with the new dog in her building. And the friend had seen the TV coverage.

Not only did Eric get Margo back, but the police raid wound up solving seven other burglaries in the neighborhood. And Margo, the now infamous twenty-pound cockapoo, got credit for the bust.

"Dognapped Cockapoo, Margo, Found and Back Home Safe and Sound! Suspect Charged in Multiple Burglaries"
—*Metropolitan Police Report.*

"Margo Goes Home: Dog Stolen in Burglary Reunited With Owner"—WRC-TV.

"Purloined pooch Margo returns to her home in D.C. after word spreads on Web and TV"—*Washington Post.*

In all, the story had been shared online thousands of times, the TV stations were all over it, and Margo quickly became the most famous dog in Washington, D.C. (sorry White House pup, Bo).

And yes, the reward was paid to the tipster. She called in after her friend told her about the reward. But this is a great story in its own right. The money went to a family who really needed it and will be able to use it to make a real difference in their lives. It took courage to rat out a neighbor, and the money was the incentive. As Bonnie and I like to say, it was a real mitzvah.

So my granddog is home safe and sound, and we all have learned, once again, of the power of the media, social and otherwise. Also friendship and community. Okay, also money, which between our household and Eric's we are lucky to be able to afford.

But the story went viral, people all over re-posted, re-tweeted, and spread the word, and for that we say thanks.

And we are the proud grandmoms of Margo Channing Peterson, the wonder dog. As Eric says, "The guy who broke into my house was implicated in seven other robberies. SEVEN. And he was brought down by Margo. I am the proud parent of one badass cockapoo."

You bet.

April 2014

I'm back from the deep South and I cannot tell a lie. While I missed my hometown terribly, I did not miss the snow you guys suffered in my absence. Since the weather icon on my smartphone always shows Rehoboth first, I got my daily Delaware news and it wasn't pretty. Well, actually, some days the pictures were pretty, but the words coming out of my friends' mouths were not.

Numerous people sneeringly spat, "You picked the right winter to become snowbirds." Yes, we did.

And speaking of snowbirds, during this winter respite I admit to having enjoyed some new-to-me outdoor activities, like birding.

My prior birding experience was limited to Tippi Hedren being dive-bombed in *The Birds*, or an occasional run-in with a flock of filthy pigeons on Sixth Avenue in Manhattan. Oh, and those French fry-thieving seagulls on the boardwalk.

But a few weeks ago I accepted an invitation to go birding at a Florida sanctuary. Decked out with binoculars, a camera, water, and snacks, we set out along the two-and-a-half-mile boardwalk through the woods.

Snacks? Even I didn't expect to need a snack for just two-and-a-half miles. Little did I know that birders move very, very slowly. They can spy a creature, stare at it for a long time with the naked eye, then look at it through binocs for an interminable period. I mean a really long, mind-numbing, turning into statues time. At this rate it would take hours to reach the mile marker, and rather than a small snack I'd need a whole pizza.

As we watch birds, all conversation is whispered, all walking is softly, with a big stick. Practically tip-toeing along, we saw buntings. These were rare and colorful winged creatures. Then we came across a huge owl, about two feet to my right off the boardwalk, just staring at us.

For the record, he did not turn his head all the way around like something from *The Exorcist*. I was disappointed. He didn't even say *whoo*. But if he did, it would have been "*Whoo* are these old people walking behind you wearing khaki, covered in badges, with cameras like AK-47s?" I wondered that myself. They were Audubon hikers looking like Scout Troop AARP.

Is it snack time yet?

I focused my binoculars on a tree limb far away and strained to see birds. Apparently there was a fabulous specimen someplace nearby, but I couldn't get it in focus. And while I may have had no prior birding experience, I have had experience with binoculars. I've used them in night boating to make certain we were looking at a red-lighted buoy and not a Coca Cola machine on shore. And I confess I've used them in New York City to watch people through the windows in adjacent apartments. Yes, it really is a Manhattan activity. Been there, done that. You see more action.

Just then a flock of large birds flew in formation overhead and everybody stared up at them, gape-jawed at their mighty numbers. Was I the only one worried about staring up open-mouthed under the flock?

Slowly, very slowly heading into mile two we saw a pileated woodpecker banging away on a huge tree, making me wonder why they don't get migraines. Then my attention slipped to Woody Woodpecker and I was off down memory lane. I was daydreaming for quite a while when I looked up and saw one member of our party gazing up at a wicked angle. Do birdwatchers get Warbler Neck or need emergency chiropractic?

I loved watching the red-crested hawks and their babies through the binoculars, but it did become a literal pain in the neck. And the pace was killing me. The only time I move this slowly is reaching for the check at a table for twelve.

We spied an enormous anhinga (yes, I have been coached on names) with a gigantic wingspan as well as a bunch of other chirping species. Lots of twitter and tweeting happened, in the original sense of the words.

And while I enjoyed the trek, and wouldn't say the morning

was for the birds, this Pileated New Yorker prefers an activity with a little more of a pulse. Like sitting at the window at 400 East 51st Street in apartment 35 F and, with my Bushnell 70s, gazing across the street into the windows of 37 C. It is the city that never sleeps, you know.

As Woody would say, "(make woodpecker laugh sound here)."

April 2014

I was all prepared to launch this column by screaming, "What were we thinking???"

That's because we just added a mini-schnauzer puppy to the family, and it's been seventeen years since we last had a puppy nursery. During this time, especially recent history, our experience has been more canine assisted living than obedience training.

Therefore, we were sure we were in for it—exhausted, hapless retirees chasing a pup, sleep-deprived seniors suffering 2 a.m. backyard bathroom breaks, and harried, hoarse-voiced parents incessantly shouting, "No! No! Bad dog!"

But those things just haven't happened. And, frankly, I'm a little pissed off. What the hell am I going to write about here?

We were in trouble from the start. After picking up the adorable, energetic pup from his parents' house, the little angel slept on my lap the entire five hours it took to drive home. No squirming, barking, biting, or peeing. "Maybe he's been drugged," I suggested.

Back home, it didn't get any worse. Dreading plaintive cries from his crate as he longed for his mommy, we did, right away, that which we'd do eventually anyhow. We let him sleep on the bed. And he did. All night, every night, not a peep nor a pee. When the alarm goes off at 7 a.m. we run him outside, where Mr. Goody-Two-Shoes does all his business instantly. Is this some kind of cruel hoax perpetrated on a journalist? I need material here!!!

Not that the puppy is catatonic, if he'll excuse the feline expression. He's all-canine, lapping the living room like NASCAR and chasing fly balls as if he's at Fenway. And you should see this little WWE wrestler wringing the necks of his stuffed toys.

But that's just it. They're his toys. Despite a home filled with enticing chair legs, delicious newspapers, fluffy pillows, leather sandals and other puppy mouth-magnets, so far there's been nary a tooth mark. We're sitting around waiting for him to turn into Freddy Krueger or Hannibal Lecter and we get nothing.

Meanwhile, the industrial-size jug of stain remover just sits, languishing. Earlier today, I became completely unraveled when he learned sit/stay the first time we tried it and, at a mere 13 weeks, actually walked to the door and barked to go out. I'm surprised he hasn't grown opposable thumbs and opened the door himself. Is this any way for a self-respecting puppy to act?

Right now, the prince is asleep under my desk, alluring computer wires free for the nibbling but he's just snoozing with his head on his teddy bear. What's a writer to do? Although the peace and quiet perpetrated by Mr. Wonderful does give me time to think about my twenty-year evolution in puppy parenting.

Our last schnauzer pups got metal food bowls, Milk-Bones, plain Purina kibble, and a wicker dog bed with an old pillow in it. Done.

Over the years, we learned of ceramic dog bowls in artistic metal holders, raised off the floor for better digestion; Tempur-pedic senior beds for healthy spines; gourmet food featuring lamb and rice; and glucosamine therapy for their joints. We succumbed to the whole expensive lot before our geriatric pets finally succumbed at ripe old ages.

But now, in the dog-eat-dog business of pet products, it's even crazier. There are more dog foods in the pet store than human brands in the grocery. And the meals are reviewed with one to five stars, with the cream of the crop advertised as natural, holistic, non-allergenic, gluten-free, carb-free, and grain-free. They are not, however, financially free. His dinner costs more per morsel than mine.

And it must be yummy, with its power protein plus cranberries, spinach, peas, apples, potatoes, beta-carotene and folic acid. I avoided the five-star food with the spray-dried chicken liver— it sounded like something my grandmother made for Passover.

There are at least 65 five-star brands from Amicus to Ziwi, and there must be a thousand dog foods in all. So now, in addition to going berserk trying to remember what printer ink cartridge I need from Staples, I can also go nuts trying to recall if I buy Blue Wilderness, Authority Mini-Chunk, or Eukanuba Gold at Pet Depot. But I did make certain to choose a food with added blueberries for brain health and memory.

Although it's not like he has to remember his social security number or a million different computer passwords. Or does he? The latest craze is interactive dog toys. We bought him the Doggy Blocks Spinner, a treat-hiding puzzle that "teaches step-by-step problem solving, in a two-part challenge!" Really? Maybe he can teach me how to use my smartphone.

Once he masters this one, sniffing out hidden kibble in the treat chambers, he can go on to the Pooch Puzzle for "circuit training your dog's brain!" Seriously, is all this necessary? Can't I just plop him down in front of *Sesame Street*?

Hang on a minute. He's not under the desk anymore. Where did he . . .? Hey, get that sneaker out of your mouth! Drop it! That's my new New Balance!

Yay!!! My kid is normal! So what if there's an incisor mark on my new footwear. It's not like it's Dolce and Gabbana. And I'm so proud he's a regular pup.

While at the moment he's just goody one-shoe, I'm sure there's more teething destruction to come. What were we thinking????

Bring it on!

April 2014

BE CAREFUL WHAT YOU WISH FOR

At first, as you know, our new schnauzer, Windsor, was an unusually docile puppy and that worried us. Turns out he was just planning his strategy.

Mostly, he's a good boy, but yesterday I uttered the inevitable, "What were we thinking?" while walking across the room with him hanging by his teeth from my bathrobe.

Windsor is teething, and his incisors are literally sharp as tacks. The new style we are wearing for spring includes Band-Aids. I just finished spraying a substance called Fooey on all our chair legs, electrical wires, and floor molding. While it might keep him at bay, he got it on his snout last night; I kissed his cheek and got the most vile and disgusting flavor on my own lips. I don't think the object of this product is to have the *consumers* running around gagging and saying, "Pfooooeeeeyyyyy!"

When Windsor nibbled a slipper last night, I told him that was disappointingly trite.

If our old house was affectionately named Schnauzerhaven for the late lamented Moxie and Paddy, our new house is now The House of Windsor.

The pup's royal name has nothing to do with stately old Windsor Castle, and everything to do with stately, eternally-youthful Edie Windsor, plaintiff in our marriage equality fight. Our boy is named for the victor in United States v. Windsor, which overturned the hateful Defense of Marriage Act. Thanks to Edie Windsor, federal marriage benefits and obligations are available to gays and lesbians married in states that permit gay marriage.

Naming the kid *Windsor* is our tip of the hat to Edie and an opportunity for simultaneous LGBT outreach. "What a wonderful name!" or variations, respond lots of folks who meet Mr. Adorable. Then, I tell them who he is named for and why.

It's interesting to see which gay and straight people immediately recognize the name *Edie Windsor*, and why she's famous, and which gay and straight people have no clue about her. It's a pretty good litmus test for who's been paying attention to current events, and, depending on their reaction, where they fall on the discrimination spectrum. As for gays and lesbians whose faces are blank at the name, wake up and smell the progress. She's a hero.

Now we need to report to our state legislators that we have a new puppy—especially those who voted "aye" for marriage equality. This is not as bizarre as it sounds, nor am I deluded to think they actually want this mundane news. But I promised.

A little over a year ago, as I testified at Legislative Hall in support of marriage equality, I described my three-decade-long relationship—our supportive parents, our careers, and how our lives mirrored long-term straight marriages but without full equality. Oh, and about our many schnauzers. The end of the testimony went like this:

"We married first in Canada, when marriage equality there became legal. We married again last year, with a big, fat Jewish wedding, recognized as marriage by our religious institution, but only as a civil union in Delaware. So neither ceremony gave us what we need most—a legally recognized marriage equal to our heterosexually married neighbors.

Now, we're retirees and sadly, just lost our remaining 15year old schnauzer. The dogs have been a benchmark for our 31 years. We urge the state to end our long run as lesser citizens. We need Delaware to pass the marriage equality bill so when the Defense of Marriage Act falls, whenever that may be, we will have the one thing we need, a legal marriage, to qualify for federal equal rights and benefits.

At the moment we're debating whether we're too old for a puppy. Our run with unequal rights has gone on long enough. Please be on the right side of history, and grant all Delaware citizens marriage equality. And we'll let you know what we decide about the puppy. Thank you. "

So I'm off to send puppy announcements to the politicians. And thank, again, those who voted for marriage equality in Delaware. Owing to our legislators, Windsor's parents are legally married, so technically he is not a little bastard.

Although after what he just did to the bathroom rug, I am not so sure.

May 2014

It's my own personal Black Friday. Time to buy a bathing suit. Yes, after the hideous winter along our shore, the sun has finally shone, and I need to go buy a sausage casing.

I started at the outlets, but the garments there are designed for skinny beach bunnies. I crammed myself into a stretchy floral number and looked like a float in the Rose Bowl Parade. Sorry—for me, orange blossoms are not the new black.

There was only one thing to do. Pay the big bucks for a "Miracle Suit." Have you seen these things? They cost as much as a three-day cruise but are purported to help you shed 10 pounds in 10 seconds. Ten seconds my foot. Seriously. It took at least 10 seconds to squeeze my left foot through the first leg hole.

Getting the rest of me inside the suit was an extreme sport. I could drop my gym membership and just wriggle into this outfit once a day.

Exhausted but hopeful, I looked in the mirror and easily saw the 10 pounds the suit shed. They were my ta-tas, bulging up toward my neck, sadly less Sophia Vergara, more Mrs. Doubt-fire.

After painfully extricating myself from that particular miracle, I tried the magic suit called "The Tankini." Ugh. The shock of seeing myself in the Tankini made me lust for a martini.

Next I tried the "Anaconda Yasmin." Yup. I looked like a boa constrictor who ate a goat. Marketing people, what were you thinking with that name???

I finally forced myself into the "Flash Dance" model. It was acceptable. Oh what a feeling.

That odious chore done, I turned to sunglasses. Even though I own several pair, every day is *Where's Waldo?* While the Ray-Ban search adds hundreds, if not thousands, of steps to my pedometer stats, it is not my best use of time. So I broke down and bought an old-lady eyeglass necklace. Face it, no matter what chic brand of shades I now wore, I was but one step away from the matching housecoat and rolled-down stockings.

I loved having my sunglasses at the ready, but now, after switching, what do I do with my regular specs? Hence, I got a second neck lanyard. The first time I left the house I swapped glasses so many times I knotted my neckware and nearly strangled. It's embarrassing being late for an event because you're cutting yourself out of your eyeglass lanyards.

So, to simplify things I bought Fitover glasses—you know, the big clunky Mr. Magoos to cover your real glasses and turn you into Elton John. But they work. Now, my five-pound sunglasses hang around my neck indoors and provide protection outdoors.

Perfect. Well, not entirely.

One day after lunch, I walked around in the house smelling an odd, unpleasant aroma. It followed me around. What the . . . ??? And then I saw it. About six inches down from my nose, nestled in the right lens of the sunglasses hanging on my chest, was a big, smelly shard of onion. From that point on, after every meal I wipe my mouth and check the lunch bucket tied to my neck.

About beach chairs.

Are they getting lower or is it me? I went to a boardwalk store with the chairs on display outside and tried out a cute little number with a drink holder built into the arm. Plop! I'm down, with my butt inches above the boardwalk, knees in my face, ready for the starting gun for the two-man bobsled.

Instantly I realized that getting me out of this chair was not a one-person job. With beach chairs on either side, I had no wiggle room. My only option involved bouncing myself forward in the chair, then capsizing the vehicle onto its side, mid-boardwalk. When you are lying in a fetal position in a fallen beach chair on the tourist-filled boardwalk, your life does flash before you.

"I'm all right, I'm all right," I hollered as I crawled out on all fours and finally stood up. Perhaps they make beach chairs with ejection seats.

My final summer prep is, of course, sunscreen. I used to use it religiously, which, for me, meant only on Passover or Chanukah.

But now I know how critical it is to avoiding skin cancer, so I have become a zealot.

But like with many obsessions, how much is enough? SPF 8? SPF 25? SPF 50? The higher the number, the more epoxy-like it is. I worry that sitting at the pool packed in SPF 50, somebody will mistake me for a plaster gargoyle. Also, does this body cement float? Might I sink like a mobster in cement shoes? Not even my miracle suit will save me.

I've decided to compromise with SPF 30. After slathering up you can still bend your limbs, but gnats adhere on contact.

So I'm set for summer. I'll cram myself into a swimsuit, don my polarized eyewear, slather myself with paste, and head to the beach. Of course, with climate change, it might be too hot to go outside this year.

If so, I can stay right here, in my pajamas, typing. It's much less complicated.

May 2014

LIFE IS WHAT HAPPENS
WHEN YOU HAVE OTHER PLANS

Oh, crap.

For the past several days I've been talking with my wife Bonnie, friends, and other writers about a dilemma this writer is in.

For almost 20 years I've been chronicling my family life in the pages of *Letters from CAMP Rehoboth*. But what if the news is not as good as getting a puppy? And, small town that Rehoboth is, word gets out when there is trouble. As a writer, what do I do? There really are only two choices. Ignore what's actually going on and write fake sunny, funny columns, or tell the truth.

For me, everything I've put in print over the years, no matter how embarrassing, silly, angry, or political has been the whole truth and nothing but. Sure, I embellish with a funny word here and there, but everything's been honest, though viewed through my skewed sense of humor.

So for me, there is only one choice—the truth, and thankfully Bonnie agrees with me.

Unfortunately, a month ago, my wife was diagnosed with cancer. It's amazing the changes that can occur to one's system in just two years. She'd had a clean bill of health in her 2012 colonoscopy. That is no longer the case. So the first message is, if you've been dragging your feet, or your ass as the case may be, get the test. Now.

Secondly, Bonnie and I are hoping to be able to make lemonade from this lemon. We will be setting up our lemonade stand outside the RV in a campground near Annapolis, MD. Bonnie is being treated at Anne Arundel Medical Center, where a dear friend of ours is a VP and in charge of her care. It makes sense.

So, throughout this summer, as Bonnie undergoes radiation, chemotherapy, and probably surgery, we will stay true to the title of this column. We will be CAMPing OUT (the actual name of

31

my column in *Letters*) in the RV five days a week and hopefully getting home to Rehoboth on weekends.

But the lemonade is not all bad. The campsite has a pool, a dog run, and even some dog agility equipment to entertain Windsor. We'll have a grill and plenty of adult beverages and will be able to entertain there. It's fifteen minutes from Annapolis for crabs and beer and lots of other diversions, including good friends.

Ah, friends. The words of comfort and offers of assistance have been many and incredibly touching. We hear you and thank you. They say actions speak louder than words, but the words have been mighty loud and lovely. One action, however, is worth a shout-out.

A quartet of friends offered to help us get the RV ready for the Annapolis adventure. Not in use since our snowy, muddy Thanksgiving trip last fall—frankly, the rig was a mess. We were told to show up on a Saturday morning to a friend's driveway, where other friends had transported the vehicle. We planned, along with some helpers, to spend the entire day in Cinderella drudgery on our hands and knees scrubbing and washing the camper.

We arrived at the appointed driveway to discover that the rig, gleaming in the sun, had already been washed, dried, vacuumed, spit-shined, and otherwise completely made over into a sparkling clean home-away-from-home. Inside our version of the pumpkin-turned-carriage there were new pillows, new runner rugs, flowers, wine (Happy Camper brand, no less!) with new wine goblets, and Rehoboth souvenir artwork to keep the beach with us at all times.

As we say in Yiddish, we were *verklempt*. Overcome with emotion, all we could do was hug our friends, wipe our tears, and ask if it was too early to get into the Happy Camper wine. It was not.

I will say that Bonnie and I intend to keep our senses of humor through this upcoming ordeal. Last week we stayed in the home of an Annapolis friend, since we don't move the RV to the campground until this coming Monday, Memorial Day.

On Thursday, Bonnie was the subject of not just one, but two separate biopsy procedures. They sedated her for the first one, did the procedure, woke her up, drove the nodding woman by wheelchair upstairs for the second go-around, knocked her out again, and went to work.

By the time I could take her to our friend's home, Bonnie was one woozy broad. She was flaked out on the sofa when my phone sent me an urgent alert about a tornado in the area. Excuse me? Exactly who is alerting me and how do they know I'm in Annapolis? Who needs the NSA listening to our calls when the weather service is watching?

Next thing I knew, that annoying beeping noise and a warning banner came across the TV. Yes, a funnel cloud was spotted in our area. Grand.

I guided my semi-conscious wife to a teeny, tiny, windowless downstairs bathroom, closed the lid on the toilet, and sat the patient down. She leaned on the wall and went right back to sleep. Then I ran upstairs for the Yorkie, poodle, and my mini-schnauzer. I'm here to tell you that herding dogs is not any easier than herding cats. I finally finished the dog-wrangling rodeo and we were all locked in the panic room together, staring at each other, wondering if we'd be going to Oz. That's when my phone issued the ALL CLEAR. All we could do was laugh. That would be me and the three dogs. Bonnie slept through the whole thing.

We finally went upstairs. The dogs let sleeping Bonnie lie. And the next day we returned to the beach in Memorial Day weekend traffic. To my knowledge, in the nineteen years we'd been visiting or living at the beach, we were never stupid enough to time things this poorly. And, as I sit here typing, I am safe in the knowledge that we have to do it all over again on Monday morning, driving the RV, towing the Jeep, and creeping back to Annapolis.

Oh, if only we could say, "Beam me up, Scotty." I'll let you know when we get there. And stay tuned for news from the lemonade stand.

June 2014

DON GARDINER WILL DRAPE IT

It's not been a great spring for us. While we were dealing with our own angst, Rehoboth Beach lost one of its most creative and loyal residents with the passing of Donald Gardiner. We lost one of our best friends.

We came back home from Annapolis this weekend for his memorial celebration, where lots of people learned things they didn't know about Don—like he had a whole early career as a Broadway dancer, that he was also a talented knitter, and that each of the friends and family who spoke at his memorial saw him from a different perspective. This was mine:

I first met Donald in 1973, forty-one years ago. I was asked to direct a benefit show at the new Montgomery Playhouse, a beautiful three-hundred-seat theatre in Gaithersburg, MD. There was some incredibly ugly baroque scenery on the stage, and I wondered how I could do a musical and comedy revue on the existing set. Somebody, I don't recall who, said "Don't worry, Don Gardiner will drape it."

In came this young, incredibly handsome guy, holding a roll of bright red fabric. He proceeded to climb a ladder and artfully drape the material so I had a brand-new backdrop. In the corner stood another good-looking young man, watching Don work. I walked up to him, introduced myself, and asked him who he was and what his role was on the playhouse team. "Oh," he stammered, "I'm Lee Mills, and I'm associated with Don Gardiner." Well, it was 1973 and nobody was really out of the closet yet.

From that moment on, I worked with Don and Lee on show after show. For years. Don was my choreographer and lead dancer in *Annie Get Your Gun*, played the romantic lead (and boy was he!) in *Philadelphia Story*, and *Bell, Book and Candle*, and designed more sets for me than I can count. From the first time Don Gardiner "draped it" in '73, he was my scenic designer right through shows we did at the Rehoboth Art League through

2003, and handling props and costumes and the almighty drapes for recent shows at CAMP Rehoboth.

During those early years we lurked in bad neighborhoods at the D.C. gay bars, and Donald refused to leave me behind one evening when they wouldn't let me into the old Lost and Found because I carried a purse. Seriously. Men and women didn't mingle much back then.

Pretty soon I gave up the purse and met Bonnie. Then the four of us walked in AIDS walks, shouted "We're here, we're queer, get used to it" in at least three gigantic marches on Washington for gay rights, colored Easter eggs, made masks and glued feathers, went to costume parties, went boating, traveled to P-town, Palm Springs, Disneyworld, and LA. We watched the Oscars together, complete with programs and quizzes made up by Donald, almost every year from 1974 on.

In the late '80s, along with all the fun, Donald set-designed our lives by designing a basement dental lab for Bonnie in our Maryland home. No slapped-up walls and doors, it had architecturally brilliant lines and stylish fixtures in the blueprints. For ten weeks, the four of us, with help from other friends, worked every single weekend and many weeknights to put up the 2x4s, drywall, plumbing, electric, and paint, so that Bonnie could move her dental lab into the space. Okay, Don, Lee, and Bonnie did the actual building. I went to the hardware store four times a day like their Sherpa.

I can still see Donald's face, when his gorgeously designed three-room, one-bathroom, basement condo became the plaster and metal dust-covered filthiness that is a working dental laboratory. He was horrified.

By the early '90s we were weekending on our boat in Dewey, having parties with frozen mudslides and martinis on a dock. And when Bonnie and I made the move to Rehoboth full-time we welcomed Don and Lee here shortly thereafter.

Don got to work his design magic as he and Lee owned and operated the Coastal Gallery and Frame Shop for several years. In retirement, Don loved his time volunteering at the Art

League's Outdoor Show, and the RB Film Festival, enjoying Cloud 9, Big Sissies, and Aqua for happy hour.

But it was hard for Donald the last couple of years. He was on oxygen full-time and pretty much homebound. As Lee became an extraordinary caregiver, Donald never complained, never said, "Why me?", never stopped living and enjoying. He never missed *Dancing with the Stars*. If it had been on TV in the '50s, Donald would have been one of those dancing stars.

Bonnie and I were so incredibly lucky to have dinner around Don and Lee's dining room table the night before Donald left us. We laughed together, told silly old stories, and thoroughly enjoyed Lee's cooking. It really was an especially lovely night.

So, as it turned out, the evening of the memorial service was the night of the Tony Awards show. How appropriate. We watched in Donald's honor. And raised a toast in celebration. I'm pretty sure somewhere, maybe in heaven or another wonderful celestial place, somebody is already saying, "Don't worry, Don Gardiner will drape it."

HAVE SCHNAUZER, WILL TRAVEL

Okay, so camping in an RV while Bonnie received medical treatment in Annapolis was a great idea on paper.

The campsite worked out beautifully at first. Bonnie, Windsor, and I enjoyed cookouts, sitting outside in our comfortable chairs and reading, strolling through the beautiful wooded campground, and hosting lots of visitors to our outdoor paradise.

Luckily, Bonnie's radiation and chemo side effects were minimal—just a little nausea, but then we could not be certain if that was from the treatment or from her being uncharacteristically in the passenger seat while I drove.

And then the rains came. Torrential. Muddy. Mildewy. The camper became a terrarium. Clean towels became scarce. Windsor became bored. We all lived in a yellow submarine.

One muddy day amid the daily deluges, Bonnie got the news she needed a surgical procedure. I made an executive decision. Fun and funky as our adventure had been, it was time for a real shower and cable TV.

So we headed to one of those "extended stay" motels near the hospital. We loaded the car with our Keurig coffeemaker, Windsor's bed and toys, and, since we had no luggage in the RV, our belongings in plastic trash bags. Our clothing filled several reusable Safeway bags. American Tourister it was not. Moving into the hotel, it was Beverly Hillbilly time.

Once ensconced, the Clampetts dried out and got ready for Bonnie's surgery.

Early morning dog-walking irony is not lost on me. We spent thousands of dollars for a fence at the new house so I could stay in my pajamas to let the dog out the back door. Here at the hotel I have to get fully dressed and run him down a flight of stairs at 6 a.m. There is no justice.

Surgery day: All went beautifully. My phone rang so often in the waiting room it sounded like a calliope. Bless you all for calls and inquiries.

I'm thrilled to report that the only real discomfort the patient suffered was trying not to laugh at her visitors' jokes. Pleasantly surprised, guests said, "You look great!" to the patient, and alluded to the fact that I looked like hell. A couple of people were more blunt.

Okay, now comes the insane part. Like I wasn't busy enough running to the hospital to see Bonnie and running back to the motel at regular intervals to give Windsor potty breaks, I decided to let the maid service have full access to our room one day. I did this by bringing Windsor to the vet for his, um, "little operation."

As luck would have it, Bonnie was released from the hospital the same day, so I spent hours running from pillar to post, packing belongings and accumulated flowers into the car for Bon, driving Patient One "home" to the hotel, then going back to the vet to get Patient Number Two.

As I lumbered up the hotel stairs, carrying the semi-comatose schnauzer, I waxed nostalgic for my old fourteen-hour work days.

So for most of a week I took care of one recuperating woman and one recuperating schnauzer. Sometimes I got mixed up about which one needed the plastic cone to keep from scratching incisions. At one point I threatened to put the plastic cone on my own head to keep me from raiding the fridge from frustration and/or exhaustion. I told a pal I was going to run back to Rehoboth for the weekend and she asked, "To get more clothes and your Smith & Wesson?"

But the good news is that Bon is feeling well, and we are facing only one more month or so here as Annapolis vagabonds. All three of us hope to be in Delaware this weekend, and we will feel less like hobos, and more like homos celebrating Pride month at home.

We'll see you on the boardwalk. We all may be eating cones. We all may be wearing cones. You never know. It's a crazy time.

DIAGNOSIS: POSTAL SERVICE
IS ALIVE AND WELL...

So we got home to Rehoboth between medical treatments, and we are on the happy road to all turning out well. The medical care itself has been expert and apparently very effective—and for that we are so very grateful.

But when we arrived home for a weekend, we got the real shocker. In what was once promised to be a paperless society, we were engulfed in an avalanche of snail mail, snowed under by a Kilimanjaro of bills from doctors, diagnostics, biopsies, surgery, clinics, radiology, chemotherapy, and an Alpine wad of confusing "explanations" from Blue Cross. Buried in bills, I hollered for a St. Bernard with a barrel of whiskey.

I'm staring at this mountainous mess and have a question. Exactly how many people does it take to change a person's colon into a semi-colon?

We've got bills from the surgeon, the assistant surgeon, the anesthesiologist, the operating room, the hospital room, the pharmacist, the butcher, the baker, the candlestick maker.

There is no end to the torrent of bills for various types of scanning. Apparently, the Positron Emission Tomography or PET scan, an imaging test that uses a radioactive substance to look for disease in the body, is remarkably effective. So good, in fact, that it often comes up with false positives. Protocol requires MRI follow-up scans of all the true or false glowing areas.

That would be scans of the abdomen, pelvis, and upper and lower colon (the actual scene of the crime), plus scans of the tonsils (seriously), lungs, brain, middle earth and upper crust.

But before doing the scans, we had to see a doctor specializing in each specific body part targeted for scanning. We saw a pulmonologist; ear, nose and throat doctor; gastroenterologist; gynecologist; craneumologist (I made that up); and more. I'm amazed they didn't send us to the country doctor who brings his old dog and long-haired Siamese to the office so his patients could have lab tests and cat scans. (Ba da bing.)

So now I've got bills for a passel of doctors and a bushel and a peck of radioactive scans, with and without IV contrast. Thankfully, all the tests except for the original problem spot turned out to be phony positives. And now we can enjoy the lovely ambience of dinner lit by the radioactive glow of my beloved.

In addition to invoices for all the scanning, we were billed for each spurt of magnetic contrast and every IV bag, injection, cotton ball, and band-aid. Expletives from the patient were free. Oops, forgot to add bills for blood counts, ultrasounds, and *conscious sedation*. Isn't that an oxymoron? If I'm a patient, I want insurance to pay for unconscious sedation.

I realize the Pentagon is famous for overpriced toilet seats and outrageously expensive nuts and bolts, but that's nothing compared to hospital bills for thermometers and ice packs. Next time I'll bring my Walgreen's digital and a bag of frozen peas.

What would cutting-edge surgery be without staples? For what they cost I could purchase the whole retail chain of the same name. Okay, that's a slight exaggeration, but the word absurd comes to mind.

For one single day of radiology alone I have a bill for therapeutic treatment planning ($826), treatment devices ($340), basic radiation ($1020—I'd hate to see what premium channels cost), special treatment procedure ($668), and finally a $750 simulation 3D. Maybe I could have given them my leftover 3D specs from *Godzilla* and it would have been cheaper.

On the other side of the medical mail mountain we have envelopes and statements from the insurance company. Don't get me wrong; I am thankful for our Affordable Care Act insurance. Much of this will be covered. However, the paperwork is staggering, with its service codes, contractual adjustments, plan allowances and deductibles. Codebreaker Alan Turing couldn't have cracked a single one of these obfuscating messages.

For each of the umpty-ump doctor's bills there is an accompanying pound of paper insurance reports. Clearly, their mantra must be "Deny! Deny! Deny!" Our first Explanation (hah!) of Benefits included a lengthy code noting "Out of Network, Payment $0" on almost every single bill. Gape-jawed and panicked, I kept myself from adding up the total debt on penalty of needing a cardiologist. But it was a *holy crap* moment. Is there medical marijuana for the medical bill payer?

Therefore, I spent the next morning, all of it, listening to tinny classical music on my landline while I languished on hold with Blue Cross. Finally, one of the supervisor's supervisors admitted to a coding error, promising to resubmit everything correctly. Oh good, double the pleasure, double the fun, double the humongous mound of mail.

My favorites are the pre-certification notices. "Authorization is solely for the purpose of advising you of the medical necessity of the requested service but it is NOT a verification of available benefits." Then what is it? Clearly it's less about the patient's life than about keeping the U.S. Postal Service alive.

We're lucky we didn't need pre-certification for me to sit at the patient's bedside days on end, calcifying, in the torturous hospital room chair. "Authorization is solely for the purpose of advising you of the emotional necessity of the requested service but NOT . . ." Do I get a contractual adjustment for a chiropractic adjustment?

So here I am, sorting through the flotsam and jetsam of the past three months. We're happy to be home for a bit, happily looking toward renewed good health in the household, and suspicious that our relationship with the postman will flourish.

If we go missing, somebody come to the house and look for us under the heaps of unopened envelopes and unsorted statements. Don't forget the big dog with the whisky. Wait! Coding error! Make that a schnauzer with a Cosmo.

THEY HATE ME, THEY REALLY HATE ME

Sitting around in medical office waiting rooms, sometimes having to watch FOX News makes me crazy. And I realize I make far-right, gun-toting, bigoted, government-hating fundamentalist religious conservatives gag. Me, specifically. I have so many credentials they hate, I'm a walking bull's-eye. It makes me proud.

Let's go with the easy ones first. As Ellen DeGeneres proclaimed on the cover of *Time* magazine, "**Yup, I'm Gay!**" With marriage equality sweeping the country, gays are the far right's boogey-people. They can raise tons of money and get gobs of supporters by frightening dumbos into believing gays are ruining their America.

Nonsense. What about that new reality show where a straight couple marry but don't meet each other until they walk down the aisle? At least lesbians wait until the second date for the U-Haul. In this reality show, if the marriage doesn't work after five weeks a bride or groom can return a spouse like a broken blender to Crate and Barrel. And *we're* ruining marriage?

I'm Jewish, which makes me even more infuriating to Sleepy-time tea baggers who want me to embrace their brand of right-wing Christian religion as the only one for the country. I actually heard, with my own ears, a Sussex County parent complain bitterly that it was wrong for the April school holidays to be called Spring Break when it's actually Easter Vacation. Easter to whom?

Telling me to find Jesus is like telling me to find a knish in Gumboro. Good luck. (Although I will admit that right wing fundamentalist Jews are just as bad as fundamentalist Christians, but that's a whole other column).

Oh yeah, **I'm pro-choice.** If I still had any reproductive choices left (Oy, has that ship sailed), I'd choose the ones those bigots hate.

Hmmm. **I'm a Northern *Elite*.** I was born and raised in New

York. I went to college. My IQ is higher than my body temperature. They hate me.

I believe in gun control. Which I also like to call gun safety. And I also believe in gun rights. But the gun lobby's "slippery slope" argument is a gunsmoke screen. They are protecting only the wealthy assault rifle manufacturers. It has nothing to do with preserving the Second Amendment and everything to do with preserving funding for their multimillion-dollar nonprofits. Without the money motive, most would agree to ban murderous battalion-killing assault weapons while letting hunters and sportspeople holster their appropriate guns. Only the survivalist nut jobs and garden variety crazies who want to kill schoolchildren don't know this. So the NRA hates me.

I believe in Social Security, Medicare, and Unemployment Insurance. Where do I start? A person I know (slightly) pontificates against "entitlements" while happily banking unemployment benefits and filing for disability. He doesn't even have the decency to feel guilty. I cannot decide whether these people are entirely heartless, just selfish, or enjoy hypocrisy. Trifecta? This whole topic reminds me of a cartoon I saw. The first panel has an anti-government protester shouting against government programs. The second panel has the man clinging to his roof in a flood, asking, "Where's the government?" Indeed.

I believe in equal pay for equal work. In 1981 in Maryland, I took a job at a company staffed mostly by women. My boss actually said, out loud, "we like hiring women because we don't have to pay them as much. When we hire a man we have to pay him more because he has a family to support." My head exploded in 1981, and in 2014 I'm still picking up the pieces. Very little has changed among the Congresspeople voting against the Fair Pay Act. If women's suffrage went to a vote today, Congress would refuse it an up or down vote and I'd be chaining myself to the Capitol steps.

But as much as my aforementioned beliefs make me America's Most Nauseous for the Snapple-Head Teacuppers, two issues in the news make me a special threat.

First, immigration reform. Several years ago I visited Ellis Island and spent an entire day feeling very close to my roots. When I told the family matriarch, Aunt Marion, about my wonderful Ellis Island visit, she laughed and said, "Didn't you know, dear? We came in illegally through Canada."

Wow. **I am the spawn of illegal aliens.** Apparently my clan went in search of a cheaper fare and better excursions on the ship from Vladivostok and wound up landing in the dead of night somewhere north of the border. They were quite pissed at having missed the Statue of Liberty. And these poor huddled masses were further baffled when they repeated their multi-syllabic name, *Onakelski*, to the border patrol and were promptly assigned the new name *Kelsey*. From then on everybody thought they were Irish Jews. But I maintain they still did not ruin America.

And finally, the far right hates me because *I love Obamacare*! It works. Bonnie was able to get insurance starting May 1 from Obamacare. Nobody ruled her out because of anything preexisting (thank you, President Obama!) and it was easy to sign up. It's good insurance, and it works exactly like any other insurance. We are extremely fortunate to have this program available to us. And, by the way, I know many other people for whom it works beautifully as well. So sue me.

Yes, I am the ultraconservative's perfect storm. And with all the time I have had on my hands lately, plus a family medical crisis to put life in perspective, I've decided that staying quiet pays no dividends.

I am woman, hear me roar . . . and vote.

THERE'S NO PLACE LIKE HOME

Ain't that the truth. After weeks in a teeny, tiny, utilitarian hotel room in Annapolis, two women and a dog have returned home to the Nation's Summer Capital, ready to enjoy the rest of the season. The good news is that Bonnie's treatment is over and we expect a good report when the docs redo the scans and biopsies in the fall. For now, we are home from the war.

It's one thing to be away eight winter weeks in Florida or up North touring Canada by RV. It's entirely another to be stashed like witness protection in a stuffy extended stay "suite" days on end, sneaking out for daily therapy appointments. Between a frequently napping patient, and a bored, teething dog, I was either comatose myself or on guard duty. At one point I was so stir-crazy I would have chewed the coffee table leg if Windsor hadn't beaten me to it.

That presented a moral dilemma. Do I place the chewed table leg up against the wall and hope the maid overlooks it, or do I leave it alone and run out the back door? Just kidding. I ratted on Windsor and offered to pay for the wobbly cheap table. I'll have to take it out of his allowance.

But while frequent bouts of cabin fever did overtake us, we did what we could to make the best of a challenging situation.

One day I visited my former Annapolis dermatologist, since here at home it's harder to get an appointment than to win Mega-Millions. I wasn't surprised that years of boating and sunshine had taken its toll and some pre-troublesome barnacles had to come off my face. I left the office resembling a speckled hen.

When we went out to dinner that night, Bonnie sat with her hospital ID bracelet on and an intravenous tube sticking out of her arm, while I looked like I'd been duck hunting with Dick Cheney. My other car's an ambulance.

At least Windsor was a wonderful distraction. One memorable

evening we came home late and had to feed the child at 11 p.m. By two in the morning, doody called.

In a sleepy stupor, I pulled pants on over my pajamas, grabbed his leash, and headed down the steps. As I hit bottom, I could see wet pavement through the glass door. That's funny, it wasn't supposed to rain. When I went out I got hit with an F5 hurricane force sprinkler system, washing my clothes and tonsils.

Drenched, Windsor and I made several passes through the sprinkler, laughing (I hope he was laughing) like kindergarteners. I'm lucky the hotel staff didn't summon a straightjacket team to take us away. Ho ho, ha ha.

And all through this adventure, we had my actress friends of 40 years or so, "The Divas" as they are affectionately known, as our out-of-town support system. Back in June, when Bonnie first returned to her room from surgery, Diva Nori, an elegant and stunning blond, was on hand. Bonnie's blood pressure hovered dangerously low, causing warning bells to go off on her monitors. Those of us in the room kept telling Bonnie to move around, shake her arms, do whatever she could to raise her blood pressure. No luck. Then, Nori peeked at her watch, announced she had to leave, kissed Bonnie on the forehead, and exited the room. My wife's blood pressure spiked. "Well, I guess I'm not dead," she said.

Oh so luckily, no. Thank you all for your support and well wishes.

August 2014
EQUALITY IS NO LONGER JUST A CONCEPT

The last decade in the LGBT equality fight in Delaware and elsewhere has been momentous. We all know the gains made, including anti-discrimination laws, civil unions, and marriage equality. Celebrations following state legislature votes were loud and proud. Weddings abounded with caterers, wedding planners, DJs, squabbling relatives, gowns, tuxes, the works.

We cheered for Edie Windsor and the Supreme Court's overturning of the heinous Defense of Marriage Act. Couples who'd been together two, three, four decades got married; young, newly-together couples married with all the requisite pomp, circumstance, first dances, and wedding-cake-in-the-face photos.

But what did this actually mean in real life? Past the ceremonies and parties, and joy of being recognized by the federal government as equally deserving the right to marry, what happened? What part of the testimony, repeated over and over for years, about the rights marriage would bestow on our minority, did I actually get to see?

A bunch.

My wife and I jointly filed taxes on April 15, as married as anybody else in the eyes of the Delaware Division of Revenue and the Internal Revenue Service. Good start.

When a dear friend lost his partner of over 40 years, he and I went to the funeral home together. After the funeral director explained the services offered, he took out some documents and asked "Which of you is next of kin?"

My friend quietly slipped the marriage certificate across the table. "That's all we need," said the somber gentleman.

How different it might have been decades ago. Actually, only months ago. There were certainly residual butterflies in my stomach. I wondered if my grieving friend would be treated with respect and given permission to do whatever was necessary to deal with the business of death. He was. But for many of us, it may take a long time for the fear and silently raised hackles to disappear.

Likewise, when my friend called Social Security to let them know of his mate's passing, we were both delighted with the professionalism of the response and the survivor benefit adjustment in his social security payment. It was one of the rights we sought in our testimony for marriage equality, now come home, in real dollars and cents.

For my part, when my wife was under medical treatment at various doctors' offices, we clearly saw a positive change in attitudes. In all matters medical, I was treated with utmost respect and spousal privilege.

Naturally this thrilled me. But not so much when one of the doctors just assumed I'd want to stay in the room holding my wife's hand for a procedure involving blood. The good news: The patient was distracted from the procedure by worrying her spouse would pass out. The bad news: I came ridiculously close to doing so.

Even in this world where HIPAA privacy reigns, I was able to take information directly from Bonnie's doctors, medical personnel, and medical billing offices. There was no phone call I could not take, or paper I could not sign.

Sure, you could tell there was disapproval lurking in the eyes of a very few people whose paths we crossed, but it was quite the exception. I found the whole experience remarkable. And though I could sense their religious or political objections, I was delighted that the law was forcing them to treat us equally. Revenge is sweet.

The truth is, so many people genuinely congratulated us on our right to get married and the fact that we had actually gotten married, we could feel the paradigm shift like an earthquake.

But giddy with equality, I knew I would eventually meet my Waterloo and figured it would be with our health insurance company. That enormous bureaucracy, with its foreign call centers and reputation for bad customer service, would be the one to burst my bubble.

Nope. When, after choosing one, two, or three from six different menus, I finally got through to a human being in Mumbai, all I had to do was say I was the member's spouse and I was given access to all the info I wanted, the status of all bills, and the specifics of Bonnie's coverage.

Of course, spousal privilege did not keep me from being stuck on hold for an eon and suffering tinny classical music. We wanted equality, and I am happy to say we are now, by law, destined to be treated as badly as everyone else.

I can't speak for other folks who have spent the last decades advocating for marriage equality, but in my legislative testimony and letters to state and national representatives, my passion was always real, but my words were often clinical. "Access for hospital visits, social security survivor benefits, 1,000 federal rights, taxation equality . . ."

While I was talking or writing, I never actually pictured sitting with a grieving friend and an undertaker or signing permission for surgery while my wife lay sedated on a gurney. And that's probably a good thing.

Songwriters Kander and Ebb, who wrote *Cabaret*, probably said it best.

"How the world can change, it can change like that, due to one little word, married."

Oh, yes.

August 2014

BIGOTS MAKE LOUSY SANDWICHES

I practically spit my vitamins across the room this morning when I realized that this coming Labor Day weekend will be my 20th Sundance Auction and Dance in Rehoboth Beach. Time really does fly, or "Fry" in my case. It seems impossible to me, but here it is, 20 years later, savoring my Sundance anniversary as well as my 20th anniversary writing for *Letters from CAMP Rehoboth*.

In 1995 Bonnie and I had just cruised into town via a two-day boat trip up Chesapeake Bay, through the C&D Canal, down Delaware Bay, into Lewes's Roosevelt inlet, and up the canal to Rehoboth Bay. Friends who also weekended here stood along the Rehoboth Avenue bridge, waving at us as we came through. Most of those folks are still our dear friends, and eventually came to live in Rehoboth Beach full-time as well.

That first summer we spent weekends living on our boat at the marina in Dewey, watching sunsets, occasionally plucking my first schnauzer, Max, out of the water, and writing my first few columns for *Letters*.

Bonnie and I, in our mid-forties, lived in suburban Maryland, where we both worked and stayed pretty much closeted except for our families and gay and lesbian friends. I'd been writing for the *Washington Blade* but I worried about losing my day job, so I wrote under a pen name. Lesbian and gay couples had great fun in those days but it was often at strictly gay events.

Even in Rehoboth, as we danced into the wee hours at our gay venues, name-calling and overt homophobia still raged. The mere thought of gay marriage was a joke.

In fact, in 1995 homophobic T-shirts could be seen in store windows and public name-calling of gays, although declining, was still popular. On one of our first weekends here, Bonnie and I went to a small hamburger place in Dewey called Colonel Mustard's. While waiting for a takeout sandwich, we overheard the owner crudely insulting the young women servers with sexist smears and making viciously cruel jokes about Rehoboth Beach gay boys.

Stunned and angry, I told Bonnie I was going to write a letter to the editor of that publication *Letters* I'd just discovered. So I did. Within a day, I was contacted by the editor who told me he was printing the letter and also meeting with the mayor, and they would both go have a talk with Colonel Mustard. They did, and although there is no data to connect the two incidents, that business went belly-up soon after.

During our brief conversation about the name-calling, Steve discovered I was a writer and asked if I wanted to write a story about our boat voyage to Rehoboth. I did, and have been writing a column in *Letters*, each issue, for the past two decades.

As a columnist I watched a lot of the world go by, from the mid-1990s through the turn of the millennium and into 2014. And I had the privilege of being able to comment on it all. From the Unabomber and his newspaper screed to that ridiculous Y2K scare where survivalists stored water in their water beds and the world waited for computers to turn into two-slot toasters. I got to opine about Monica Lewinsky's blue dress, the whole Clinton impeachment circus, the Bush-Gore election debacle, and the horror of 9/11. I covered Delaware's eight-year quest for an LGBT anti-discrimination law, followed in remarkably short order by a civil union bill, and then the snowball rolling downhill to marriage equality.

Less globally, I covered splattered gourds at Pumpkin Chunkin'; the first and now 17th Rehoboth Independent Film Festival; surviving summer traffic; a sugar high at Chocolate Fest; and the vision for, planning, and realization of the dream for a CAMP Rehoboth Community Center.

Readers said they related to my grappling in print with real estate travails, technology, AARP, various phone companies, call centers in Bangladesh, health care, applying for Social Security and Medicare, recreational vehicle trips, cataract surgery, and the whole process of aging gracelessly by zip-lining.

Personally, I have written of living in one boat, two condos, two houses, one RV, and with one pet BMW and four schnauzers. I've been sprayed by a skunk, cultivated a bat colony, transported rescue dogs, and reported on innumerable do-it-yourself disasters. Oh, and chronicled our two marriage ceremonies.

I've loved every minute and I'm not done yet. I just think it's appropriate, at this 20-year mark, to thank CAMP Rehoboth for the marvelous privilege of penning approximately 300 CAMPout columns. It's been grand and I hope the best is yet to come.

And like the "It Gets Better" campaign for gay youth, life in Rehoboth Beach keeps getting better and better, too.

Who's laughing now, Colonel Mustard?

September 2014

Smartphones have changed everything. And I'm as addicted as anybody else. But I realized it was out of hand last week when a bunch of my friends came over to my house to play with their cell phones. Well that's what it seemed like, with everyone intermittently peering at their devices.

When somebody remarked at dinner tonight that the six of us must be special to each other because nobody even brought their cell phones to the table, I knew trouble lurked.

Let's face it, what we have here is the good, the bad, and the ugly.

Under the good category, smartphones are fabulous. How did people find each other in the quiet ages at Pride parades or Poodle Beach without iPhones? And they are great for communicating instantly without actually having to talk to anybody. Not to mention the joy of carrying an 18-volume Funk and Wagnall's Encyclopedia in your pants. There's no arguing that a device that can reroute you around a five-mile traffic backup or instantly settle a dispute about who recorded the doo-wop classic "In the Still of the Night" (The Five Satins) is very, very valuable.

More importantly, think of all the good that cell phones could have done had they been invented earlier. I'll bet passengers on the Titanic would have liked the captain to have gotten a text from a nearby boat saying, "Look starboard."

In films alone, Maria could have warned Tony to stay at the drug store because Chino was gunning for him. And, as Cary Grant loitered atop the Empire State Building thinking he'd been stood up, somebody surely would have called to tell him Deborah Kerr had been hit by a bus on her way to him.

Imagine if Celeste Holm called the gas station for a couple of gallons of gas so that bitch Eve Harrington didn't get to go on as Bette Davis' understudy in *All About Eve*? Life-altering.

But frankly, useful and fun as smartphones are, most of us, myself included, have become needlessly boorish and rude because of these amazing devices. In fact, I was severely chastised recently, and rightly so, because I unthinkingly answered a call while my companion was mid-sentence. It was rude, I admit, but I hear the ring and turn into one of Pavlov's dogs. I've always considered myself a pretty polite person and I am appalled at my behavior.

So . . . I checked online at the Emily Post Etipedia (seriously). It seems I'm not the only one who's been led into loutishness by a smartphones. Legions of us have to learn to behave better.

Therefore, when out in public, I'm now going to try to keep a ten-foot distance between me and anyone else whenever I talk on the phone. Face it, nobody wants to hear me answering my phone and saying "Yes, I picked up the biodegradable toilet paper for the RV." Likewise, sitting at breakfast at Crystal, I don't want to hear the guy behind me discussing his date's nipple jewelry.

And I know I was giddy when I discovered I could download a snippet of "There's No Business Like Show Business" for my ringtone, but I will now revert to a less intrusive sound. After all, while there may be no people like show people, everyone else at Browseabout would probably prefer not to hear Ethel Merman. Ever.

Also, as of today I will make it a new habit to identify myself when texting to people who might not have my number stored in their phones. Many times I've been pinged to read "meet me at Mixx at 6?" or "were you scandalized by Showtime's Masters of Sex tonight?" and I have to type "um . . . who is this?" So embarrassing.

As for those pings themselves, I will try to turn the sound off and just glance at my screen occasionally. I'm telling myself that we don't have to be available 24/7 even though it's technically possible. I've been in a room when a cacophony of pings erupt and I'm always saying to the person next to me "Was that me or you?" Seriously, I have to learn that texts don't always require an instantaneous answer. I may meet my Waterloo with this one.

A corollary to the pings is the *swoosh* of sent mail. If a person you are talking with turns their back and you have a second to send an email, the *swoosh* they hear may sound like you are passing gas. You'll want to avoid this.

And finally, when I am engaged face-to-face with others, at the bank or shopping, I promise to give them my full attention. I am not awfully guilty of texting or talking in the checkout line, but last week as I answered a text and smiled at the cashier, I inadvertently donated money to some charity that does not share my values. Oops.

So, as I obsessively check in on Facebook, text my friends, consult Trip Advisor, and answer any call that comes my way, I will try to be more polite about it and enjoy the good, try to avoid the bad, and be certain not to behave like the ugly.

I promise to practice better cell phone etiquette. Is there an app for that?

September 2014

I've been a volunteer in my day, but as far as I know this is the first time I have ever acquired a volunteer. And it's free-range and flowering in my front yard.

I'm talking about, of all things, an unsolicited bushy beanstalk thingy that sprouted in front of my house. After being gone for several weeks this summer, we came home to find our petunias trampled by a wild leafy plant with blossoms and little green balls.

Dumbfounded, as we don't have 4-H clubs in Manhattan, I posted a photo of the mysterious greenery on Facebook. "What the heck is this? " I queried.

Answers ranged from zucchini or squash to Venus Flytrap. When, overnight, the largest green ball turned burnt orange, I had my answer. It's the Great Pumpkin, Charlie Brown!

Just call me Farmer Jacobs, cultivating a bona fide pumpkin patch spanning the front of my manufactured home. How much farther from Fifth Avenue and 54th Street can I possibly get?

But how did vegetables sprout on my lawn? I consulted the *Old Farmer's Almanac*, frankly, the very last book—even behind *The Wit and Wisdom of Richard Nixon*—I ever thought I'd read. In the book title *Old Farmer's Almanac*, is the almanac old, or the farmer? I want to know whether to be insulted or not. But I digress.

The venerable *Almanac* said the plant was a "volunteer," meaning it wasn't planted there on purpose and probably came from seeds gusting into my north forty from somebody else's pumpkin patch. Alternately, it could be, get this, deposited by a sea gull airlift. Really? We all know what sea gulls deposit on cars just back from the car wash and it's no stinkin' pumpkin seeds.

Then, it hit me. Did I plop a pumpkin in front of the house last Halloween? I flipped through the zillion images on my iPhone and, sure enough, last October we had a seasonal tableau with a big fat pumpkin and two baby pumpkins in the front mulch bed.

Since benign neglect is my landscape plan, like the attention I give all my shrubbery, I just left it there to fend for itself when we wintered in Florida. Apparently the gourds decomposed and come summer, squash!

Once the mystery of the origin of the species got solved I asked myself, now what? Wikipedia said pumpkins are "widely grown for food and recreation." Either I channel my inner Barefoot Contessa and bake pumpkin pies (highly unlikely) or gather my gourds while ye may and enter that Delaware classic, Punkin Chunkin'. Actually, that IS about as far from 54th and Fifth a person can go.

Every day I would visit my personal pumpkin patch. Each night I would troll the Internet reading up on the care and feeding of my bumper crop. Mind you, I never actually did anything recommended, as I was too busy surfing the computer, but I had great intentions.

Ergo, one day, as I stood admiring the homegrown produce, I noticed a white powdery substance on some of the leaves. Uh-oh. My familiarity with white powdery substances has been limited to powdered donuts and well, um, let's leave it at that. It couldn't be either, so what was it?

The *Almanac* announced I'd contracted Powdery Mildew. Well, not me personally, but my crop. The good news was it might make the leaves turn yellow and drop, but it would not hurt the pumpkins. The bad news was that leaf loss might expose the pumpkins to sunburn. Seriously? Do I spray them with Banana Boat SPF 30?

Again, I sought agricultural advice. Turns out I could use an expensive fungicide, which sounded hasty to me, or simply wash the leaves with mild soap and water, like a fine sweater. I chose the latter, bending over to hand wash my plant, my rear end to the street, looking for all the world like one of those lawn ornaments of the old lady bending in the garden. The effort was not attractive, but it was successful.

So here it is, almost October. I plan to harvest the homegrown pumpkins for Halloween, ready for carving or cooking. Or, most likely, just looking. But I will leave one good gourd out in the mulch pile to decompose and incubate for next year.

Just think of the potential volunteer armies we could have if I rotated my crops. Would rotting marshmallows bring Easter Peeps? Might discarded strawberries bring strawberry fields forever? Would decomposing grapes spring forth a vineyard?

"Pumpkins are fine, but I'd rather have wine."

—Fay Jacobs, *Old New Yorker's Almanac*

October 2014
AN ATHLETE OF OLYMPIC PROPORTIONS

Well, I failed to enter the Delaware Senior Olympics for another year.

Several friends enter annually and this year they came home as Pickleball medalists. The game's name alone makes me want a pastrami sandwich. But I understand it's big with athletic seniors who bow just a bit to age. Pickleball combines half-court tennis with flailing ping pong paddles. I know better than to step in front of that speeding bullet.

But every fall I look at the Senior Olympics registration form, searching for something I could possibly enter. There should be a category for just filling out the paperwork, then making a two-pointer chucking it into the circular file.

The list of Olympic events, from A to Wii, just brings me back to my sordid athletic history.

The flashbacks start with archery. In addition to my theatre and journalism classes, I needed three college credits in physical education, so I went to the archery range. Thankfully it was a pass/fail grade and you passed as long as you didn't skewer the instructor to the bull's-eye. Have you tried to draw back a bow and shoot an arrow without scraping your forearm with the taut bow string? I would have aced the course if I'd been graded for the size of the hematoma on my wrist.

My basketball career was short. I played back in the day when women had to stay on half the court, guards in the back, only forwards could shoot, and everybody wore unflattering apron pinnies over their street clothes. It was a look. In junior high, the first time I got under the basket to take a shot, an Amazonian schoolgirl blocked me with her meaty fist to my chin. I spent the rest of the season at the dentist.

I guess I could have played bocce, which I enjoyed once with friends who had a bucolic farmhouse and plenty of turf for a court. I came home and instantly bought a bocce ball set in an attractive attaché-like case. I dragged that never-opened bag in and out of four houses, two condos, one RV and my manufactured home before it went away at a yard sale.

Once, over 30 years ago, trying to impress the athletic person who became my spouse anyway, I tried biking. Days after purchasing a K-Mart special, we biked 25 miles from Easton to St. Michaels in Maryland. Fortunately, it was totally flat terrain.

Using my college acting skills, garnered when I wasn't slapping my arms silly at archery, I used chipper conversation to mask my panicked wobbling. We completed the schlep and followed up with cocktails and Preparation H. Ow.

Thinking me a biker, my honey planned a cycling trip to Nantucket. I have to admit to feeling smugly superior on the ferry, when others were in cars and I was decked out with bike, backpack and a tiny rear-view mirror on my glasses.

And then we docked. The cobblestone streets could shake loose a kidney. And there was a humongous paved hill straight up to our hotel. Instead of planting a flag at the summit I planted my bike and walked all weekend. When we got home I hung the two-wheeler on hooks in the garage where it rusted to the wall and was conveyed with the house.

Moving right along, Olympic choices include alien sports like horseshoes. The only actual horseshoe I ever saw was nailed to the hoof of a carriage pony on Central Park South. Racquetball was out because the concept of four walls, a hard rubber ball, and me just screams detached retina. And the Track and Field category is based on running, jumping and throwing, things I only do when I see a large spider. And the shot put, javelin, and discus throw events must be sponsored by rotator cuff surgeons.

Then there was volleyball. At summer camp at some lake in Connecticut I spent what little time I was not at theater rehearsals on the volleyball court. I practiced mostly duck and cover moves, but I was pretty good at punching the ball on my serve.

My career ended in the summer of '62 when I got under a spiked ball with my whole hand but took the brunt of the hit with my middle finger. For the rest of the summer I wore one of those metal and foam rubber finger splints and wound up permanently giving everybody the bird. Not how to make friends and influence campers.

The truth is, golf might just be the only sport where I have a snippet of credibility. When I first picked up a set of clubs eight years ago, the idea of my taking up a sport was so hilarious to my friends they all wanted to play in my foursome. How horrid was I? I aspired to "riders"—shots hit far enough to warrant riding in the cart to retrieve them. I was the league clown in a league of my own.

Then, I improved just enough to ruin my game. As a garden variety bad golfer, I was no longer a novelty or so amusing. Besides, the wordsmith in me couldn't overcome the contradiction in the term *par*. Why is below par on the course a good thing and feeling below par after a night of martinis a bad thing?

Conversely, if being above par means better than average, why is taking ten strokes instead of two to get the green not a good thing? Semantics ruined my concentration.

So I'm still a spectacularly horrid golfer, although I do play if I want an afternoon in the sun communing with baby bunnies. But there's certainly no golfing at the Olympics in my future.

As my New York Yankees say, there's always next year. Perhaps 12 months of practice might ready me for Wii bowling or shuffleboard.

In the interim I guess I will just have to content myself with the Triathlon. Type, Edit, Proof.

October 2014

With Halloween just around the corner, I visited a pop-up Halloween Spirit shop, looking for an outfit for my dog. After all, the pet parade is this weekend. I also needed some inspiration for costumes for me and my wife, as we never miss the opportunity to bar hop in Rehoboth on Halloween weekend.

As I trolled aisles filled with monsters, superheroes, and a disturbing array of bloody body parts, I flashed back to ghosts of Halloweens past—and lessons learned from them.

First, select a costume that does not make your spouse hate you. Back in the '80s at a D.C. party, I knew we'd dazzle the crowd with our two-person camel costume borrowed from a local theatre production of *Joseph and the Amazing Technicolor Dream Coat*. We won first prize, but the rear end of the camel didn't talk to me for a week. And I had to pay for her chiropractor.

Next, be mindful of your ability to dazzle while still being able to eat and drink. Reference the previous example. Only the person in front of the camel's hump could sip and chew without disrobing.

One year we attended a penthouse party with a fairy tale theme. Let's face it, almost all of the fabulous fun events and costume parties we attended back in the day qualified as "fairy tale" evenings. But this party requested that the fabulous fairies and their dykey cohorts come as costumed Cinderellas, Rapunzels, or evil queens. There were always a couple of garden-variety evil queens in street clothes making snarky comments, but that made the parties even more fun.

The costume winner that year was Snow White, in an authentically designed and hand-sewn Disney outfit with perfectly coiffed black wig, enhanced by this man's perfect black beard. Sadly, though, he had his waist cinched within an inch of his life and could not eat a morsel. A Grimm choice. Ba-da-bing. I think Bonnie and I stretched the theme a little by going as Peter Pan and Captain Hook. Okay, that might have been the "Movie and TV Musical Theme" year. The details are lost to Father Time. But Bonnie donned her little green Mary Martin lezzie outfit (MM was one, you know) and I got dolled up like that famously flaming Captain Hook. And yes, Cyril Ritchard who played Hook was gay, too.)

That time Bonnie got to take full advantage of the catered buffet and flowing beverages while I tried to balance a plate on my elbow and a martini in my hand without gouging people with my big plastic hook.

So, having learned my lesson, we went to a subsequent party—TV theme—as a grape-stomping Lucy and Ethel from *I Love Lucy*. We wore wigs and peasant dresses, painted our feet with purple food coloring, and were done. We ate and drank unfettered.

The next lesson is to ignore judgmental young store clerks. Just a few years ago, friends here at the beach hosted a 1960s hippie party, which sent dozens of folks to one of Rehoboth's two hippie-era clothing stores for tie-dye and wearable blankets. I guess we got there late in the week because I overheard a clerk actually say, "Here come some more old people for tie-dye."

And they weren't even evil queens.

I can't remember the year, but it was when that kids' show *Teletubbies* featured a purple creature called Tinky Winky, wearing a triangle on his head and carrying a red purse. The American Family Association hyperventilated about the character looking "gay."

Well, they may have castigated him in Utah, but here in Rehoboth we celebrated him. I showed up on Halloween at the Blue Moon dressed like Tinky Winky (hands free for cocktails!) and so did several other revelers. All the Tinkies were here, were queer, and the American Family Association never got over it.

Standing in that Halloween Spirit store I realized that growing older is mandatory but growing up is not. The rumor is that if you haven't matured by age 50 you don't have to. I'll drink to that, especially if my costume allows me the freedom to do so.

I'm just as excited about Halloween this year as when I was eight and dressed like Roy Rogers, or thirty-four and sharing that two-person camel. Only now I'm older and wiser. I will make sure my costume is fun but minimalist, with no orthopedic dangers or impediments to feeding myself.

Oh, and Windsor will go to the parade dressed simply, as well. He'll want to be free to forage for boardwalk French fries.

Actually, this year I may just wear a plain half-mask and my T-shirt with the words, "People don't stop playing because they get old; people get old because they stop playing."

Happy Halloween.

November 2014

LETTING GO AT THE PET PARADE

It was the perfect match of motive and opportunity. I had an adorable one-year-old Chihuahua who needed a forever home and it was time for the Halloween Pet Parade.

But I suppose you're wondering how this schnauzer-identified writer came to be seeking a family for a homeless, pointy-eared Chihuahua child.

My friend Sally's daughter, in a misguided fit of kindness, took in the homeless pooch. An apartment dweller who works long hours, said daughter was in a situation that didn't work for her or the pup. So Sally decided to find the dog a new home, enlisting unsuspecting us in the scheme.

"What's her name?" I asked.

"I have no idea," answered Sally.

Okay, then. Off we went with our schnauzer Windsor and little Miss Anonymous. For the record, young Windsor, in the throes of puppyhood, was just to be a spectator at the parade this year. He could decide for himself if he wanted to dress for success next time. Good thing, as our hands were full of Chihuahua.

At the start of the boardwalk, with hundreds of two and four-legged parade contestants lining up for the stroll, we realized the daunting nature of our mission. Yes, the participants in this boardwalk empire were all certified pet lovers, but almost everybody already had at least one ridiculously costumed dog, and many had two or three. The throngs of dogless spectators seemed satisfied with their status as well.

"Isn't she cute!" exclaimed an admirer, "What's her name?"

"Lady Gaga," I said, a little too quickly.

"She needs a home," Sally said. The admirer backed away.

When a young woman stopped to pet Rita Mae, Sally tried again. No sale. Not that we were selling anything. The bright-eyed, affectionate Yoko would certainly be free to a good home.

By this time the parade had stepped off, with dogs dressed as witches, goblins, tacos, and pumpkins. One golden Lab was a prison guard, with his female humans doing a tableau of *Orange Is the New Black.*

Clever!

Meanwhile, Billie Jean kept attracting oodles of attention.

"Is she housebroken?"

"I think so," said Sally, "but we've only had her two days," she added, for truth in advertising.

I have to say, the dog was precious in a demure, quiet way. Of course, for all I knew, she could be Lizzie Borden, temporarily silenced by the surrounding stimuli. And there was craziness: Viking babies in strollers with dogs in Wagnerian armor; teacup pooches in bomber jackets; tuxedoed men with bride and groom poodles; pint-sized prisoners and pit bull pirates; retrievers in Dalmation costumes; Dalmations as great white sharks.

All the small dogs in strollers reminded me of comic Karen Williams's disgust at seeing people pushing pups in carriages along Commercial Street in Provincetown. "People!" she admonished, "What are you doing to them? For pity's sake, they're descended from wolves!"

With the Chihuahua still homeless at this point I understood we had to work fast.

"Maybe you'd like to hold Martina," I offered one onlooker, wondering if we could just hand her off and run.

A float carrying a castle, with a royally dressed Boston terrier mouthing the words to "Let it Go" rolled by and I thought if only we *could* let it go.

At one point, a family huddling on a white bench looked at Whoopi and said "Awww." Sally launched into her script. Actually, the family seemed quite interested, with lots of questions, discussion, and an exchange of phone numbers. Promising!

Then we ran into a local animal advocate who suggested we call the shelter the next day, as they might have a home available for Mata Hari. Small dogs were in demand, he told us. Good news indeed.

With the parade having passed by, unsuspecting marks became

less ample. It looked like Mariska might be ours for the night. Then, a kind-looking woman and her husband happened by and glanced our way.

"Isn't she adorable!" the woman exclaimed, "What's her name?"

(In unison) "Alicia Florrick." "Olivia Pope."

As Sally went into her song and dance, the couple became intrigued, noting that their elderly Chihuahua had passed and they were ready for a new family member. Might it be our very own Cagney or Lacey?

After assuring the interested couple that Princess Di may or may not have had her shots but that she was certifiably affectionate, we made sure to ask for their credentials as well. After all, we wanted to be sure Hillary would be going to a responsible, loving home. With all of us satisfied with the answers, we heard the magic words. "We'd love to take her."

Yes!

And as Meryl or Lady Edith or Sappho herself rode off into the sunset, two adoring parents making a complete fuss over her, we breathed a sigh of happy relief. Let it go, let it go, that perfect girl is gone!

Windsor, intent on sniffing out dropped boardwalk fries, never even noticed we were one Chihuahua down. And frankly, I was impressed that the boardwalk itself was still tidy, no dogs having done their own interpretation of letting it go.

Then Sally got a text from the family who'd been interested in the pup a half hour before. "Sorry," Sally texted, "we found a home for her." Wow. We might have been able to adopt her out twice. Maybe more than that. A good day's work!

As for Windsor, he managed to find a dirty half sandwich on the boards.

"Let it go!" I sang.

January 2015

LIKE PEAS IN A PODCAST

In case you've been under a rock like me, a podcast is a 21st century radio show. But unlike a Norman Rockwell painting of a family gathered around the radio cabinet for a 1943 episode of *The Lone Ranger*, a podcast is downloaded to your computer, MP3 player, or iPhone for personal listening.

Oddly, podcasts are the rage for everyone from twenty-somethings to computer geeks to old farts like me who have been painstakingly instructed on getting and retrieving podcasts on our smarter-than-us phones or other devices.

Oddly still, the whole thing is not so different from those 1960s transistor radios we listened to in the dark ages, for music now labeled golden oldies. My 12-year-old self had a tiny earphone with a wire dangling to the plastic mini-radio in my pocket as I listened to hottie (not that the term was invented yet) Bobby Rydell. Today, it's exactly the same, except we have earphones on both sides of our heads.

Most odd of all is that a particular National Public Radio podcast, called *Serial*, has been holding an entire nation's ears hostage for months now. If you haven't listened to this wildly popular series yet, you are not as *au courant* as you think. Turn off your Walkman and get down with this podcast.

Serial is composed of a dozen installments by reporter Sarah Koenig, telling us about a 15-year-old Baltimore murder. And how she may or may not think the teenager convicted and incarcerated for the crime did it.

With cool sound effects, interviews, and the reporter's tortured flip-flopping on the jailbird's guilt or innocence, this tale volleys back and forth between did-he-or-didn't-he so many times Dramamine should sponsor this drama. The convicted murderer is now in his 30s, still maintains his innocence, and, frankly, may get another look at his case by the courts because of the fuss *Serial* caused.

How much fuss? There are hundreds of blogs, tweets, and Facebook pages plus numerous dueling podcasts devoted to listener comments and theories. Amateur detectives nationwide are now working the case. *Serial* has eclipsed the Kardashians on the blogosphere. Radio, for heaven's sake.

But as fascinating as the case is, the really fascinating thing is that people are all sitting around, not just in cars, but in living rooms and at computers, listening to that wireless thingy Marconi invented in 1897. Although it is true that you need the latter-day inventions of computers, iPads, iPhones, and iSpeakers to listen to it. It may be radio, but it doesn't come out of one.

So here I am in the car, driving to Florida, my spouse at the wheel. I'm holding the iPad between us, listening to the episode "The Alibi," with each of us craning our necks and ears trying to hear the not-quite-loud-enough iPad speaker.

It's Best Buy to the rescue with an external iSpeaker . . . much better. But the car's gearshift looks like a snake pit with coiled black cords everywhere. Wireless? Not so much. The iPad's connected to the cigarette lighter, the speaker's connected to the iPad, the iPhone's connected to the auxiliary cigarette lighter, and my shin bone's connected to my knee bone.

And, absolutely nothing is connected to the car's in-dash radio. Pretty soon cars will come without radios but with 16 cigarette lighters. Even though nobody smokes anymore.

Frankly, my mate and I found *Serial* so gripping we wound up just off I-95, in the parking lot of a South Carolina Best Western listening, transfixed, for an added half-hour before heading into the motel for the night. The last time I spent an extra half-hour in the car before going into the house it was the backseat of a '65 GTO with a prom date during the Bobby Rydell era. And for me, this time was much more interesting.

So now we are all Pod People like the characters from *Invasion of the Body Snatchers*. I just learned that this podcast revolution has been going on for a decade without me, and there are thousands of episodes for me to download at will.

It's all a product of our new on-demand world. I can watch

my favorite TV shows one week at a time on TV or on demand, all at once, on my iPad; I can listen to *Serial* one week at a time on NPR or download the dozen podcasts to gorge on it hour after hour, on demand, on my iPhone. If I go for my morning walk, I can demand more stories on my little tiny iPod. This on-demand business is pretty convenient.

Well, it may be an on-demand era, but one thing they haven't invented yet is a way for my columns to write themselves on demand. iWish.

February 2015

It's great to be back in print after the winter hiatus. Especially so I can share some things I've learned over these chilly winter months.

First, I learned we really do get by with a little help from our friends. The number of folks asking after my wife's health both warmed and invigorated us. And we're thrilled and thankful to report that after months of treatment, Bonnie has been declared cancer-free. Whew! And thank you all for your healing thoughts and concern. We love you.

Secondly . . . I learned that while I drink socially and love my Cosmos, I am not an alcoholic.

How? Because on our celebratory cruise out of Port Baltimore we bought the all-inclusive Royal Caribbean drink package, which cost almost as much as the cruise itself. We rationalized it would be easier to pay up front, order cocktails without thought to wallet, and avoid being staggering drunks with a staggering bill at the end.

Well, it worked precisely as planned. The second we boarded the ship with our traveling companions, the four of us ordered the Drink of the Day in a souvenir glass, festooned with little umbrellas and an aquamarine liqueur that turned my tongue blue.

From there we enjoyed Bahama Mamas at the welcome party, top-shelf martinis before dinner, wine with our food, and more booze at the trivia contest. Nightcap anyone? Why not? It's "free."

By morning, there were breakfast Bloody Marys, then a second Bloody at the pool, an afternoon beer at the art auction, and a magical cocktail convoy from drink to drink to drink through dinner, a show, and music in the lounge.

"Well, we're certainly getting our money's worth," we joked, as we carried on, well-oiled and having a blast. As the casino slot machines consumed our quarters we consumed innumerable beverages and lurched off to our cabins—whether the ship itself was doing any lurching or not.

With our little all-inclusive EZ-Passes dangling from lanyards around our necks, we could belly up to the bar day or night with impunity. Which we did, savoring mimosas, martinis, Cosmos, 12-year-old Scotch, mojitos, a rum swizzle, the occasional gimlet, and a random chocolate martini or two. This march of the mixed drinks went on for four decadent days.

By day five I whispered to the waiter to hold the champagne and serve just the orange juice. A Diet Coke with lunch tasted amazing. Come happy hour we were back to ordering a round of vodka shots. It's 5 p.m., do you know where your liver is?

In unspoken accord, we all cut back, having just one drink prior to dinner and just one glass of wine with the meal. While we played trivia in the lounge that night, no further alcohol touched our lips.

Now I'm not saying we became members of the Temperance Union. However, over the next two days we paced ourselves, not letting the urge to score a financial coup on the drink package overtake our good sense. The ship's special farewell drink was three ounces of no-name rum with two scoops of raspberry sherbet in a sippy cup. We just said no to that drug.

It was all oodles of fun, we got our money's worth, and I thank Royal Caribbean for conclusively proving that while I do not have a problem drinking, I do not have a drinking problem.

I also learned that booking an inside cabin can save money but not your sanity. Traveling overnight, from the Port of Baltimore to Cape Canaveral, I set the iPhone alarm clock for 7:30 a.m. and hunkered down for a night's sleep at sea.

Windowless, we were in a quintessential black hole when the alarm rang. Bonnie and I popped up, turned on a light, and dressed to hit the deck, all set to knock on our companions' cabin door and head for breakfast. I put my watch on. It had stopped at 3:40. Ugh, damn batteries. I grabbed Bonnie's Swatch. It said 3:41. And the second hand was still sweeping. *What the hell?*

"Um, Bonnie, there's a problem. The alarm went off, but I don't think it's morning."

"How would we know in here? It's like being in a dungeon," she said.

I checked the phone. It read 7:42 a.m., GMT. It was morning alright, IN LONDON, at Piccadilly Circus. In our sea cave it was still 3:42 a.m.

Apparently, even though we were cruising from Baltimore, USA, to Florida, USA, we'd crossed into international waters and my too-smartphone changed to Greenwich Mean Time. Very mean. So, all dressed up with nowhere to go for five hours, we got back into bed in our clothes. Next time, at least a porthole.

And finally, I learned that somebody my age who parties like a twenty-something, drinks like a fish, and gluttons out on all that rich cruise ship food, comes home with gastritis. I'm lucky it wasn't gout.

So now I'm on another kind of liquid diet, prepping for an endoscopy and colonoscopy. I have to say "cheers!" with that disgusting procedure prep beverage. It sure could use a shot of no-name rum and a dollop of sherbet. Bottoms up!

February 2015

Just yesterday, after the gym, I couldn't think of the word for the angle you boost the treadmill for increased huffing and puffing. You know, the hill thingy, the degrees up, the doohickey button . . . I didn't know if my cold sweat was from the exercise or the fact that my brain had logged off.

A half-hour later the word incline popped into my head, the antithesis of the decline in my cognitive function.

I thought it was just me, but every Baby Boomer I know is losing their nouns. And there's only so many times you can use "the whatchamacallit" in a conversation. It's hell waiting around for the disappeared.

According to WebMD (and we all know to trust the Internet!), normal age-related forgetfulness starts to happen after age 50 and it's nothing to worry about. But it's no picnic, either. It's like my brain goes on hiatus mid-sentence and I have to wait for Lassie to come home.

And proper nouns are the worst. I just saw a wonderful movie with John Lithgow and, you know, what's-his-name, the actor from, oh crap, what was that movie, the one where he was the painter Diego Rivera married to Frida Kahlo, that's it, *Frida*! But I still couldn't horkle up the actor's name. In case you care, I looked it up, and it was Alfred Molina.

Sometimes I can see an actor's face before me, recite his entire resume, tell you more about him than his agent can and the name is still MIA. You know, *Silver Linings* guy, he was in that movie about the congressman taking a bribe and he had a perm, and now he's in the biggest first-weekend grossing movie ever, and holy moly, what's his damn name? I give up. It will probably come to me at three in the morning, after deadline on this column.

It's not just famous people. I hesitate to spill my dirty little secret here, but I've had trouble remembering people's names for years.

In fact, my problem with names may be compounded by all the same-gender couples I know. It's a heck of a lot easier knowing that one part of a straight couple is Teddy and the other is Alice, than remembering who's Ben and who's Jerry. See my problem? I call it "Gaylexia."

I can get by with the generic "Hi there!" only so many times, deceitfully appearing to know everyone. I cover my disability in various ways—eavesdropping until a name comes up; enlisting trusted friends to whisper names in my ear; or proclaiming, "Well, if it isn't Trouble" when confronted with a couple whose names have gone missing.

This afternoon I had to go to the grocery for a whatchahoozie, that green thing, not an artichoke, aw c'mon Fay, it's round, well sort of round, and all I could think of was artichoke, and I started sweating and stuttering, with the word on the tip of my tongue. I know the size, texture, and city of origin of the damned thing but not its name. The people at Super G thought I was completely nuts standing in the produce section, doing a happy dance and hollering "Avocado!"

So goes my life without nouns, my daily game of fill in the blanks. Frankly, I think it's worse than it used to be because our brains are packed with a zillion passwords, plus cholesterol numbers, security codes and, around here, thanks to the new 911 system, five-numeral house addresses. Our hard drives are full. It would be nice if we could go to Staples for added memory.

I also blame memory lapses on the coma-inducing music on hold, on the phone. I can't tell you how many times I've zoned out and completely forgotten who I'm waiting for. When they come back on the line I pray for a clue in the first sentence. It's hell wondering if it's the plumber or the gynecologist.

Hold on, I'm getting a reboot here, a news flash, here it comes, total recall, it's Bradley Cooper!!!! Of course, *American Sniper*! That was quicker than usual. But still stressful, and of course, they say stress adds to your forgetting your words so this is just one vicious, um, round thing, hoo-hah, thingamajig, circle!!!!

And as I was hemming and hawing, fishing for that vanished

noun, I flashed onto, oh you know, the great actor from Gump, married to Rita Wilson, c'mon Fay, for pity's sake, um, Kennedy Center honoree, ummmm . . . Tom Hanks, that's it! I saw him in an eminently forgettable film once (so bad I never tried to remember the name) where he was a premed student and he flunked a test because he couldn't remember the name of a particular body part in the alimentary canal. Try as he might, Tom couldn't come up with it.

After leaving the exam, he was back outside on campus, when he suddenly had an epiphany and shouted, both as expletive and quiz answer, "Rectum!"

I feel his pain.

OMG, my tongue is numb. I knew thath what wath thuppossed to happen but . . .

I'd had my first drink of kava. Heard of it?

Kava is some kind of South Pacific pepper plant. Its scientific name is *Piper methystickum*, which is how you sound if you drink kava and then try to say "Messy stickum," which is actually what the liquid looks like in the plastic cup.

A friend and I stumbled upon a Kava Bar, thinking it was a coffee bar in a coastal Florida town that shall remain nameless. The slogan for the little beach town is Keep (name of town) Weird, and after a sip of kava I began to see why.

We were searching for a standard iced coffee, and instead were introduced to kava by a barista who told us you don't drink it for the taste, you drink it for the effect. He mentioned euphoria, relaxation, and mental clarity. That sounded good until he added, "Actually, it tastes like muddy water and will numb your tongue."

That ringing endorsement should have been enough to curb our kava curiosity, but nooo, we said we'd sample some, on the promise it was good for us, would cleanse our liver and would make us sleep well.

This last promise bothered me, as it was 9:30 in the morning.

"Yes," the kava barkeep swore, "the drink's Latin name means intoxicating."

Okay, so he was saying I could just as easily smoke weed or knock back a Bahama Mama for the same effect as chugging a liquid that looks like the contents of the bucket after you wash your car. What's this all about?

A chalk-written sign in the establishment noted that kava is a drink made from the roots of a plant that has been used for centuries as a ceremonial and recreational drink and is mostly consumed in cultures like that of Polynesia, Hawaii, and Micronesia, to name a few places I've never been. It is touted to elevate your mood and cause talkativeness. It is often used to treat social anxiety.

I do not have social anxiety but I was beginning to get anxious all the same as three very social, hippie-ish gentlemen converged behind the bar to toast to the kava virgins. They each hoisted plastic cups of the hooch, not their first of the day I suspected, and grinned at us. Donovan's "Mellow Yellow" pulsed from the speakers.

According to these mellow fellows, kava is to be consumed as a group activity, launched with the hearty toast "Bula!" which either means "to long life and good health," or "you schmucks just paid money to drink sewage."

"Bula!" they chanted as my friend gulped the odd brown liquid, curling her lip a bit, but soldiering on. For some reason, when it was offered to me, I took a gulp as well.

It tasted like somebody mixed chocolate YooHoo and Febreze. And that's when my tongue went completely numb.

When offered more, I answered "No thangth."

Then, after my friend finished her cup of sludge, came the warning. "Oh, and don't mix kava with alcohol; you'll feel sick."

Oh, no! We were on our way to watch an Orioles spring training game, which surely could not be accomplished without beer.

Exiting the kava bar, we went next door to the coffee shop we thought we were going to in the first place. There, we ordered actual large javas to wash away the kava's gritty aftertaste. We kept waiting for something interesting to happen but nothing ever did. I didn't even seem extra talkative, although my pal said "How would we know?" I don't think it was a compliment.

On our way to the ballpark I googled kava. In the South Pacific the plant is used not only as a recreational drink but for everything from treating leprosy to use as a surgical anesthetic. It can be chewed, ground, or pulverized.

And, of course, there were Google ads for the stuff hawking "Premium Hawaiian Kava, direct from the farm, ships same day!" You can even get convenient capsules of kava, presumably to avoid the sludge factor.

But then came the warnings. According to WebMD there are big health concerns about kava causing liver toxicity and damage. You are supposed to stop taking it immediately if you develop jaundice or other symptoms too grisly for mention in a family magazine. It has already been banned in Germany, Switzerland and Canada. *Oy!*

But I wasn't really concerned. During our ceremonial slurp we didn't swallow much of the evil pepper root. Besides, from our seats in the bleachers, while the Orioles lost to the Minnesota Twins, we gamely sweated out any residual kava. The two ice-cold beers and a hot dog chaser worked their usual magic.

While we were not feeling especially mellow, the good news is we weren't turning yellow either. *Bula!*

Later that night, as we walked past the Kava Bar, we saw that the sign touted "Kava, a way of life!"

Maybe in Bali H'ai, but not for me. I'll just have a Bloody Mary, thank you.

March 2015

WILL IT BE 50 SHADES OF FAY?

I now make a plea for help and assistance. And you could even win dinner out! Here's the scoop. After a dozen years as author and publisher, I'm going on the stage. That's right, in my dotage I'm breaking into show business.

I've put together a reading, an entertainment, an afternoon or evening of stories based not only on my books and columns, but on some personal history and more than 35 years in the fight for LGBT equality. The idea for this project came from my years of attending writers' conferences and reading my stories in classes, at organized readings, or at happy hours. Lots of colleagues urged me to put together a "show," so here I am.

As Billy Joel sings, "you may be right, I may be crazy," but it's happening.

So far, I have performed this nascent "thing" twice for fellow writers/critics and we have been work-shopping the script to get it right. And I thank my writer colleagues for being so constructive and willing to work with me to make changes.

I've done some readings in Florida and have an evening scheduled in the Carefree lesbian community in Fort Myers at the end of this month of March. The upshot is that I've got two short acts (with an intermission for cocktails!) based on my insistence that nothing is ever so horrible if it's worth the story you can tell—and that includes the closeted 1980s, discovering Rehoboth, fighting against discrimination and for equality, not to mention surviving the scourges of zip-lining and puppy training.

So here's my challenge to you, dear readers. I need a title for this gig. And I need it fast. This reading will be presented in Rehoboth for the first time in May and ad deadlines beckon . . . so what is this thing called?

Originally, I named it *Fried & Prejudice: A Funny Thing Happened on the Way to Equality* . . . but that title was fun only if people knew my book titles. Besides, the show is about lots more than just the fight for equality.

At a recent dinner a pal suggested calling it *50 Shades of Fay*. When we got done spitting our Cosmos across the table, we figured that one might have a short shelf life. We could call it *Aging Gracelessly, One Story at a Time*, but I don't think it conveys the whole picture.

So that's where you come in. I want title suggestions emailed to me. There's dinner for two at stake. Oh, and tickets for the reading, whatever it's called, will be on sale beginning April 1 at camprehoboth.com.

Yes, April 1 and I guess I'm the April Fool.

April 2015

It's true. *Letters* readers are a clever lot. Also generous, as so many of you wrote to me over the past month to suggest titles for my new project—now officially named *Aging Gracelessly: 50 Shades of Fay.* Yes, that was my pal's Cosmo-fueled joking suggestion, which, as it happens, stuck.

But other suggestions, very descriptive, exceedingly clever, and perhaps too long or too insider to work as an advertising graphic, made opening my email a blast all month long. But in fact, some are so good I may use rotating titles for subsequent bookings! Readers, I cannot thank you enough for the effort!

There's not enough ink or word count to list them all, but here are some of the entries by deadline time: *Faybles!*—I love this, although I'm not sure it would help advertise the show. Perhaps it could be *A Sop's Faybles.* Is sop a word?

Ashes from the Fray, which certainly describes this old activist, perhaps *Ashes from the Fay.*

As I Fried, Drank, Screamed and Aged in Rehoboth—a title which covers the subject more closely than I care to admit.

From the *Closet to the Coast: Four Decades with Fay and Friends*—a damn good description.

Fayme: She's Gonna Live Forever—a truly scary thought. Oh what a feeling.

Baby, I was Born This Fay—thanks, Gaga fans.

Oh, that's so Fay—as shouted in the school yard.

So title suggestions are still coming in. And the reading itself is being fine-tuned and rehearsed. I did an evening in Carefree Resort in Ft. Myers—the first time before a really large crowd, and I am happy to report that I survived. In fact, I had a grand time and it was reported to me that the audience did, too.

I'm walking a fine line here between trying to promote this reading thingy and not coming off as a shamelessly self-absorbed old poop. But my wife reported that I got a standing ovation at

Carefree. It's odd that when you are on stage, a place I am unaccustomed to being, you don't even notice those things. I was too busy trying to get the hell off stage without tripping down the steps.

So, the truth is, I'm getting inquiries about doing the "show" (it's a reading, not exactly a show, but anybody got a better way to describe it?) at events from P-town to New Orleans. So I gotta keep going, performing, and fine-tuning.

If this is aging gracelessly, I'm all for it.

April 2015

I love kayaking except for two things: getting in and getting out.

My first adventure was on a tributary of the Bay of Fundy. As my mate and I schlepped toward the river bank, dragging two heavy kayaks behind us, I was already questioning my sanity.

Then, at water's edge we dropped the vessels into the bay and mine started to leave without me. When I hurriedly stepped into the boat with one leg, the kayak launched itself downriver, pitching me backwards, and slamming me down into the kayak cockpit like Whack-a-Mole. Both my hips and thighs took hits, while my right leg hung over the side, dragging along like a rudder. By the time all of me was in the boat, I realized my paddle was still on shore. Yes, I was literally up the creek without one.

As my spouse's boat neared and we made the paddle hand-off, bruises had already popped up on my hips. But I was eventually able to relax a bit and try paddling. Surprisingly, I could propel the craft forward without tearing a rotator cuff.

It was peaceful on the water. For a while there, kayaking put the fun back in Fundy.

But, of course, we had to come back. And while we were gone, the infamous Fundy tides had receded, making the path to our launch site a quarter of a mile of murky sludge. When I tried to extricate myself from the boat I couldn't pry myself up. Clearly my bruised hips and thighs had swollen a trouser size larger from the entry wounds.

My struggling inevitably tipped the kayak and I capsized into the sea of brown goo. That sucking sound was me lifting my head up, my Ray Bans staying behind. At least I was able to sink my hands into the gunk and drag myself, on my belly, out of the kayak and crawl the 30 yards towards shore. Staggering up onto the bank, I was a half-dead ringer for the *Creature from the Black Lagoon*.

For some reason, in Nova Scotia, we kayaked again. Our guide told us to get into the boats from a standing position in knee-deep water. This time, I fell in just as badly but much, much faster, thanks to the insanely frigid water.

When the instructor described a safety maneuver to right a flipped boat, he called it the "Eskimo roll." Fat chance of my being able to do that. I'd be going glug-glug with the fish, doing a sushi roll.

But I have to say, the scenery on this trip was gorgeous, kayaking along rocky inlets and stunning vistas. Although for the whole adventure I obsessed about having to get out of the damned boat.

And the resulting experience lived up to my fears. Once again I couldn't dislodge myself on my own, so I did a reverse Eskimo roll, leaning over the side and sliding out of the boat, landing on my hands and knees in six inches of chilled water. I got a glacial facial and complimentary hypothermia. For future reference I should restrict kayaking to warm water venues and hire a personal trainer to haul my ass out of the boat.

Glutton for punishment, but in a warmer climate, we most recently joined a dozen women of a certain age kayaking on a Florida canal. As we all got ready to launch our boats, we were given little square seat cushions with sturdy handles on two sides.

"We'll use them later to help get you up out of the kayaks," our guide said. "They're called Lady Lifters." Wow, clearly I was not the only one who needed a new exit strategy. I might, however, have been the only one thinking it was a sexist name for the little pillow with handles. Offensive name or not, I knew I'd appreciate the assist. As for getting into the boat, at least there was now a padded seat when I came crashing down.

We explored the canal for two hours, enjoying the tropical foliage, blue herons, ibis and what appeared to be a floating meat loaf, but was actually a manatee.

Along the bank we spied an enormous snoozing alligator and I paddled by with as little gusto as possible. This was no time for premature eject-u-lation. When the gator opened his eyes and took a step toward the water I froze, but mercifully he stopped in his tracks. We were paddling toward our lunch stop and I wanted to eat lunch, not *be* lunch.

After a wonderful afternoon, we returned to the boat ramp. When it was my turn to disembark, two muscular women waded ankle deep in the water, to either side of my kayak. They each grabbed a seat cushion handle and on a count of three lifted this lady up and toward shore like Queen Victoria in a sedan chair. Success!

Knowing that a dry landing is now possible, I'm ready to tackle Rehoboth Bay and the canal to Lewes.

But first, do you know anyone who can take an old seat cushion, sew extra-strength handles onto it and make me a Person Lifter?

Then I'll be ready to rock and roll, Eskimo or otherwise.

May 2015

Thanks to generous friends who had time-share points to use or lose, Bonnie and I recently wound up with five free nights at the decadent St. Regis Hotel in New York City.

The St. Regis, at Fifth Avenue and 55th Street, is the most gratuitously luxurious hotel I have ever stayed in or will be likely to stay in again. In fact, the accommodations were so stupefyingly self-indulgent I felt guilty: How can I enjoy this when people are homeless and starving and . . . Well that lasted about a minute.

My not using the complimentary butler service or not plunging into the 800-thread Egyptian cotton sheets was not about to solve world hunger. Although I was stunned that the actual cost of the room would have been more than a dollar a thread count per night. But I dove right in anyway.

The next morning, our wake-up call was a real person instead of a digital robot, saying good morning to us by name—although our friend with the time-share points booked the room, so our butler called us by her name, which is a little unsettling when you first wake up.

The butler arrived with our coffee (one with cream and one with soy milk as requested), set it down on the coffee table (under the Waterford chandelier), and asked if he should pour it for us. By all means. Oh, and he brought back the shoes I'd put out the night before for polishing. It may have been the first time the staff polished dilapidated Clark's clodhoppers. Now they looked new.

Each day we also got a complimentary fruit basket, an ice bucket refilled several times a day, and a newspaper of our choice. Favorite touches included the lavish bathtub, shower and twin sinks, along with plush bathrobes and fuzzy slippers. The replica Louis IV bedside tables had phone-charging stations on the side.

But my fave by far was the television embedded in the bath-room mirror, like magic, no frame, no dials, just an image that eerily comes up on the mirror when you push a button. I watched a PBS fundraiser with clips of Ethel Merman singing "There's No Business Like Show Business" while brushing my teeth.

This whole hotel experience flew in the face of our usual experience. We go for cheap and clean, saying "how much time do you spend in the room anyway?" But this time we spent a lot of time lounging in the room, forgoing the nightcap or early walk for more time to luxuriate. Was the room $735 a night better than the Sleep Inn or Motel 6? Yup.

Of course, our free stay had its downside. We had to hoof it to breakfast at a bagel place down the street because the hotel menu offered the lowly plain omelet at $42. A jumbo mortgage was required for French toast. The service charge alone for room service would buy a delicious breakfast for two at IHOP. A glass of orange juice in the dining room was $4 more than a glass of orange juice AND Grey Goose at favorite watering holes.

Did you know that the Bloody Mary was invented at the St. Regis in 1934? Or so they claim, but I believe there are dissenters, like Harry's Bar in Paris. However, we read the history of their bartender concocting the drink but calling it a "Red Snapper" because the name *Bloody Mary* was just too vulgar for the time. I read the tale but didn't taste the official hotel signature drink because it was $25, making it much too vulgar for me. I got one in the theater district for eight bucks.

And this hotel is so over the top there's an employee in the lobby just to push the revolving door for you. God forbid you should move a muscle.

Once out in the street we could see a huge change in the city since our last visit. It was now completely Uberfied. There seemed to be fewer private cars and even fewer yellow taxis than ever before. But the streets teemed with big black sedans and SUVs, all of them working for Uber.

We loved just calling a car from our smartphones and having somebody pick us up within minutes, charge the ride to our credit card, and in lieu of requiring a tip, ask for a simple 1-5 star rating. It was great. Although eight million people are all standing in front of buildings squinting at black cars to see if they are Toyotas, Suburbans, Cadillacs, or whatever their iPhones tell them is coming to get them. Frankly, with all the black vehicles, the whole city looks like it's at a funeral.

We did a lot of fun things for five days, like getting half-price theatre tickets, strolling through Times Square, getting our fill of corned beef on rye, and then going from the ridiculous (champagne cocktail at The Plaza) to the sublime (hot dog cart lunch in Central Park).

We even spent a fun morning at Madame Tussauds—hobnobbing with waxy celebrities who would expect their friends to stay at the St. Regis. We had a grand time. But all good things must end, as we checked out of the lush life and headed back to the trailer park.

May 2015

Oh, goody, it's Older Lesbians Month. Well, actually it's Older Americans Month, but several LGBT organizations are celebrating it as Older Gay and Lesbian Days—like gay days at Disney, only this one is celebrated at Outpatient testing. Or perhaps Walgreens, at the corner of kvetching and complaining.

Hell, for me, every day is older lesbian day. Why, just this morning I found out exactly how old, when I got a text from Overstock.com telling me my cheap dining-room chairs had arrived yesterday.

That's weird. They weren't on my porch last night. Or this morning. Then I read the email noting the chairs had been delivered to our old address. A place we have not resided in for the past seven months. Never mind my chatting up somebody in Dubai twice last week to make sure that didn't happen.

Who said you can't go home again? By 7:20 a.m. Bonnie and I were headed for Old Landing Road and our former residence. Pulling up in front, we saw the three enormous cartons on the stoop. Please, I thought, let the people who purchased our place be weekenders.

Luckily, nobody was there as we celebrated our personal old home week by dragging the heavy cartons off the stoop, onto the driveway, and into the Jeep. The wheezing alone was enough to create a neighborhood disturbance. These geriatric burglars on one last heist were fortunate the police didn't cruise by. "Old Lesbians Nabbed in Driveway Drive-by!"

Returning to the trailerhood, backs already aching, we got to repeat the athletics in reverse, plus drag the unwieldy boxes up the stairs and onto the porch—where I had paid good money to have them delivered in the first place. There is no justice. There is, happily, Bengay and a heating pad.

So we're celebrating being old lesbians. Part of Old Lesbians month online was a shout-out to OLOC, the group "Old Lesbians

90

Organizing for Change," a terrific national organization committed to empowering old lesbians. Check out the group if you don't know it. Very cool old people.

As for being those old people, laughing helps. The other day I was back at Walgreens; is it irony that I get most of my exercise picking up prescriptions? Anyway, I tried to pick up my prescription. It was nowhere to be found. The pharmacist and the clerk forgot where they put it. After fifteen minutes of standing there, shuffling back and forth, and hearing them take three phone calls and a pharmacy consultation with another customer, I started to laugh.

"Why are you laughing?" asked the pharmacist.

"Because," I said, "You're screwing with my anxiety medication. It struck me funny. You couldn't lose the cholesterol pills?"

Pretty soon we were all laughing.

Actually, that's a good thing about being an old lesbian. I feel I have license to speak my mind even more than I used to. Look out. This old lesbian is just one martini away from an inappropriate comment or a verbal rampage. It's kind of fun.

I am an old lesbian, hear me roar. Now where did I put those pills?

May 2015

Sometimes we exit our comfort zone for a good cause. In the name of animal rescue I attended a Paint Night charity event.

How bad could Paint Night be? Every time I ask myself that kind of question I have flashbacks from unfortunate experiences like zip-lining or learning to two-step. Outwardly, at least, this event seemed less risky.

Halfway through I started to understand why Van Gogh cut off his ear. Look, there's a reason I paint with words, not acrylics. I am fine art challenged.

I learned this at age six when I dipped a paintbrush in water to "paint" in a special coloring book where the water turned black and white images to blue or red. Anybody old enough to remember this?

With exquisite eye-hand coordination I flipped the water bowl onto the book, painting all the pages simultaneously, flooding the coffee table and removing the lacquer finish from the tabletop. It was not the kind of masterpiece my mother anticipated.

Even crayons got me in trouble. There was a 1950s TV show where you could send away for a piece of see-through plastic to cover your TV screen and use a crayon to color on the TV with Winky Dink. No, I am not a savant, having remembered Winky Dink's name all these years. I googled "crayons on TV screen." And there he was.

But I do remember coloring with Winky when the plastic fell off and I continued to express myself on the RCA picture tube and onto the adjacent living-room wall. Again, my art led to family attention, and not the good kind.

Here's a random fact: The Internet reports that the aroma of Crayola Crayons is the third most recognizable smell for adults, right after coffee and peanut butter. I get that. In fact, I just got up from the computer to go sniff a crayon, which for some reason I actually had in my office. Coffee smells a lot better.

But back to my art history. Apparently, scolding from my early artistic endeavors left me brush-shy from kindergarten all the way through Medicare eligibility. I knew better than to try and paint, color, or draw anything, ever.

I even flunked Pictionary, with people guessing that the Thanksgiving turkey I drew was a BMW with a quirky hood ornament.

My mate won't even let me paint the walls in our house, which, of course, is no hardship at all.

But I digress. Paint Night. We arrived at the host restaurant, MIXX in Rehoboth, to find 30 or so tabletop easels, each holding a blank canvas, with a paper plate on the table featuring black, white, bright green, and bright blue paint blobs.

What? No burnt sienna or magenta?

I ordered my first martini and faced the blank canvas, preparing to unleash my inner Leonardo da Vinci. Perhaps I'd channel Georges Seurat, painting *Sunday in the Park with George* as *Tuesday in the Bar with Fay*. I couldn't wait to get creative.

That's when I found out we'd all be painting the same swimming turtle picture, with step-by-step instructions. So much for my delusions of grandeur. I ordered a second martini.

Now I have to say, between the drinking, laughing, and painting we all had a total blast. I did my best, enjoying slapping paint on the canvas while trying not to splash it into my nearby Grey Goose.

After nearly two hours of monkeying with the thing, the final result was supposed to be a turtle, surrounded by coral and seaweed, with sunlight rays sparkling through the water. Oh, and little fish swimming by.

Mine showed a rhinoceros or possibly the QE2, surrounded by dildos and linguini, with white shoelaces hanging in the blue stuff. Oh, and little hand grenades swimming by.

To my left, across, and behind me were recognizable turtles in lush coral and seaweed-enhanced seas. Mine, not so much. You'd think I'd been sniffing crayons. Clearly, my half-century moratorium on fine arts endeavors was a good thing.

And following tradition, despite the apron I was given to keep me clean, I ruined a great pair of shorts and gave my running shoes random blue highlights. Luckily, this time, I spared the tabletop and did not paint on the restaurant walls.

When it was all over, we applauded everyone's efforts and cheered at the money made for animal rescue. And we were cautioned to be careful with the still-wet canvases.

It wasn't until the next morning I noticed the two-inch black acrylic blob on the door of the Mercedes. I'm sure I have some Goof-Off in the drawer with the crayons.

For Andy Warhol, his muse was a soup can; for me, it's the garbage can. But at least we raised some money for the animals.

June 2015

There are days I hate the U.S. Postal Service. Today was one of them. Now before I go all postal about it, some history.

I was in my late forties when it started. Targeted mailings. Those creepy, very specific, unsolicited offers where it's clear that somebody with a mailing list knows your exact age. The first, of course, was the AARP.

That was a shock. At 49 they wanted me to join an organization with the word *retired* in its name and pay $8 a year for the privilege. I wouldn't retire for 15 years yet, the nerve! But I can be bought. So I gladly accepted the mantle of retired person to save on hotels and rental cars. I'm vain, not stupid.

But I always flashed my membership card for the discounts, certain they would think me a liar if I applied on face value—my face. It was a sorry day when a clerk stopped me from foraging in my wallet, saying "I believe you ..."

The next targeted assault came several years later with random solicitations for long-term care insurance. Here I was, mid-50s, working hard and playing hard, and they had me drooling and debilitated in a nursing home.

Just reading the stuff was debilitating. What 56-year-old wants to think about needing assistance with daily activities like toileting (is that even a real word?), bathing, dressing, eating, and incontinence care? I was both horrified and impressed by their scare tactics.

"43% of those needing long-term care are under age 65. You may need it now!"

"At this rate of increase, ten years from now, a policy for a 50-year-old would cost 50% more than an equivalent policy for a 50 year old would cost today."

Good grief, that last sentence could cause brain damage all by itself.

Day after day unsolicited insurance offers poured in. It was effective weight training just to haul the enormous pile of junk mail to the recycling bin on my way to the dance club.

The long-term care game went on for years, supplanted only recently by the tsunami of solicitations for supplemental Medicare insurance. Known as Medigap policies, these offers buried my mailbox in an avalanche of waste paper unequal to anything suffered before.

Every insurance company in the country sells a policy, and every 64-year-old I know is a victim of the onslaught. With Baby Boomers coming of Medicare age at a frightening rate, these offers singlehandedly must be saving the venerable old Postal Service.

And it's not just in the mail. Technology targets us by age on Facebook. "Are you 64 and looking for a Medigap policy? Click here!" I even got a pop-up ad on my Kindle. If I'd been reading the Anti-Aging Zone or Wrinkle Wars, I'd understand, but I was reading a novel full of drugs, sex and rock and roll. What gave them a clue?

I thought about it. If hundreds of insurance companies know my age and exactly how to find me, why the heck should we worry about the NSA spying on us? They should just ask Mass Mutual or John Hancock to cough up their data.

Of course, before I put my own John Hancock on any of the hundreds of offered policies, I had to perform due diligence and compare and contrast them. If I'd been retired since age 14 I still wouldn't have had time for all that. So in the end I went with my old friend AARP. After all, we've been an item for 15 years.

But did the mail stop? Nooo. We've gotten personalized solicitations to get our hearing tested, use discount coupons for a full-body MRI, and quite annoyingly, dozens of ads for cute cottages in senior communities where graduation means a bed with railings in the nursing home. Make it stop!!!!!

Now we're getting a gift catalogue for curmudgeons featuring easy-up toilet rails, power seat La-Z-Boys, coccyx cushions, and full-page magnifying readers. How did this happen? I may not order much from Sports Authority or Boater's World anymore, but I can still get out of a chair by myself. I should be getting Travel catalogues and Wine of the Month Club solicitations, not offers for living-room ejection seats.

I've got so many coupons for incontinence products I'm seriously pissed off. But today was the very worst. Yes, dear readers, I opened my mailbox today to find the holy hell of targeted marketing inquiries—a personal invitation to pre-plan my own cremation. Hot damn.

I stared at the invite, incredulous. And I couldn't toss it in the trash fast enough as I left the house to go kayaking. They're just going to have to wait a while, hopefully a long while, until I catch up to the marketing dolts eyeing me with their direct mail campaigns.

In the meantime, I do think I'll check out a wine of the month club and a trip to climb Machu Picchu. No pressure stockings needed.

June 2015

What comes around, goes around. I've heard that a million times, but I think I really experienced it one day a week ago.

I opened Facebook on my iPhone and saw a friend request from a name I recalled from long, long ago. I didn't really know this person, but had met her a lifetime ago, as I was peeking out of the closet in, oh my gosh, it must have been 1981.

I remember going to a strange (for me) neighborhood in D.C. to a place called "The Women's Center." I knew it was a meeting place for lesbians and that scared the heck out of me. But I went, talked to some women, and signed up for an all-lesbian evening cruise out of Annapolis for the following week. In 1981, this kind of thing was a very rare event indeed.

On the night of the cruise, all I wanted to do was be inconspicuous as I parked my car at the City Dock. Omigod, I locked my keys in the car (nervous much?), had a passing policeman call a locksmith, and drew the kind of attention (in my mind, anyway) I had hoped to avoid. I remember staring down at the sidewalk wondering if passersby could see the neon sign on my back saying "lesbian."

Finally, I timidly walked onto the tour boat. All around me were female couples and groups of women friends, animated, laughing, talking to each other, and the discovery of all this rocked my world. And yes, it was a lifetime ago.

Would I fit in? Make friends? All I could do was stand against the rail of the boat and watch the evening swirl around me. I also recall being introduced, in passing, to a woman who intrigued me—for her confidence and comfort with herself and the surroundings. Me, I was timid, frightened, and unsure of everything in this new world of gay women.

So, back to the future. Last week I got this Facebook request. I clicked "accept" and sent my new FB friend a message.

HI. Fay Jacobs, here. Weird question: do you recall if you were on a tour boat (the Harbor Queen) out of Annapolis sponsored by the long-gone Women's Center of D.C. back in the dark ages 1981ish? If so, it was my first participation in any kind of lesbian event—I was closeted and so very afraid . . . and I believe I met you that night and thought to myself "I want to be like her—out, and proud." I don't know how we became FB friends, or where you know ME from, but I just wanted to share this memory with you. And I am proud to say that it took a while, but I am out, very proud, and a lesbian writer, and activist. Go figure! Thanks for the inspiration.

My computer blinked with a response.

Hi Fay . . . you really made my day! Thank you so much for your lovely message. It meant the world to me. I indeed remember the Harbor Queen and the Washington Area Women's Center . . . those were the days! How long ago . . . don't I feel old! You certainly are a kindred spirit . . . be proud that you took the risks you took . . . and thank you for YOUR involvement in our community as well. Perhaps our paths will cross one of these days. My partner and I do make it to Rehoboth once in awhile . . . Feel free to keep in touch and thank you so much again for your kind words! Maybe I'll see you on the Supreme Court steps in June. We will definitely be there for the announcement!

I wrote back.

Wow, our memories are pretty good for old lesbians! We'll try to meet you on the steps of the Supreme Court!

It's funny the turns life takes and what the now-ubiquitous world of social networking can do. But it's also true that none of us has gotten where we are (or where we still have to go) without the help of great organizations, activists, and pioneering women (and men!!!) who helped create the progress we enjoy today.

Which brings me to an upcoming event here in Rehoboth by one such organization fueled by several such marvelous activists. It's an LPAC (teamlpac.com) meet and greet event for the opportunity to have cocktails and conversation with the group's leaders, and some spectacular Delaware politicians.

LPAC is a nonpartisan Political Action Committee with the mission to build the political power of lesbians by significantly affecting the election of candidates who champion LGBTQ rights, women's equality, and social justice. LPAC Board Members Hilary Rosen (one of my favorite lobbyists and TV interviewees), Karen Dixon, and Executive Director Beth Shipp will be on hand to meet and greet, as well as to promote LPAC's mission and key initiatives. Check out teamlpac.com for details—and help make history!

As for me, I'm certainly not the terrified, closeted young woman I once was. But I bet even in 2015, with all the progress made, there are many women like that, still hesitant to come out, still afraid of that neon sign with the L word on their backs.

Let's hope the efforts of groups like LPAC and our own CAMP Rehoboth and local PFLAG chapter can make a difference to them, and ease their way.

As for me, I'm glad to have the neon L on me. Light it up!

June 2015

Now I'm a hunter-gatherer.

I was in the Florida Keys with friends—me to spend three days in the pool and my mate to go deep-sea fishing with Captain Bob.

On the night before our first respective outings, my other half ordered the catch of the day at a local restaurant. Apparently, it was the catch of the previous Tuesday, as food poisoning ensued.

With no way the first mate could leave the condo the next morning, I offered up my non-fisherperson services instead. I couldn't promise that my being crew would be better than fishing alone, and, frankly, it might prove way worse, but I was oddly game and so was the captain.

We saw a glorious sunrise, applied a thick coat of SPF 50 epoxy, and tore through the calm ocean at warp speed until we were, gulp, 39 miles offshore, no land in sight. I expected the inverted hull of the Poseidon or at least Leo DiCaprio to float by.

Alfred Hitchcock's birds circled overhead, but I learned they signaled fish below. Captain Bob lowered the baited hooks and we trolled. Within minutes, my fishing rod began bouncing and I answered the call to "reel it in!" Sadly, I turned the reel handle backwards and it fell off. I avoided Bob's gape-jawed gaze, scrambling to screw the handle back on so I could claim my still-hooked catch.

Back in business, I reeled the bright blue and yellow mahi-mahi in toward the boat. When it was swimming alongside, Bob grabbed the pole and told me to get the net into the water to scoop up the fish. I leaned over the side of the boat, stretching mightily, the net barely touching the waves. "Put it down in the water!" the captain urged. "I'm trying!" I hollered, poised for a Greg Louganis into the sea.

By the time Bob, who is six foot four, with a 747's wingspan, realized I was height-challenged, he was holding the flapping fish up shoulder high and just airlifted it into the boat.

A fish gobbled the bait on his side of the vessel and Bob, going solo, reeled in and netted a second and then a third mahi, making it abundantly clear this was fated to be a one-man operation with a studio audience. I did my best to stay out of his way. We snagged plenty of too-small fish, tossing them back, but at regular intervals the royal "we" caught the big ones.

Working to remove the hooks, the captain drew lots of fish blood, turning the boat into a MASH unit. It took everything I had not to scream like a girl. We hosed down the ER and, given the hot sun, doused ourselves as well. It was my first ever wet T-shirt event.

Overall, we spent seven hours finding seagull-approved fishing spots. I only snagged the boat's prop twice. Final count: 11 legal-sized mahi-mahi. The captain deserved a citation for overcoming somebody like me aboard.

I freely admit I fled to the pool when it came time to gut and clean the catch of the day. I am what I am. But our fresh fish dinner, prepared by our hostess, was astoundingly delicious. Adventure over, right? No.

After my spouse recovered and spent two more days catching mahi-mahi with the captain, we prepared to transport 35 plastic bags of flash frozen fish filets onto the plane home. We were to pack them in a cooler, with less than five pounds of dry ice and explain we packed the cooler ourselves. Simple.

While my mate returned the rental car, I wheeled my cooler to the baggage scale. "What's in there?" asked the airline official.

"Mahi-mahi with less than five pounds of dry ice. I packed it myself," I answered, obediently.

"Show me," he said, "because lady, you know you are asking us to transport dry ice and it's a dangerous gas."

This guy was giving me dangerous gas. I untangled the cooler strap, lifted the lid, and expected the clerk to nod and send the seafood onto the conveyor belt.

"Take the dry ice out and weigh it," he ordered.

You're kidding? I considered, then rejected, offering him a fish-stick bribe. Then I gingerly extracted the dry ice sack, hoping it wouldn't leak and cremate me as I carried it, like a live hand grenade, to the next scale. 4.4 pounds. Whew. I cautiously retraced my steps with the potential terrorist weapon and plopped it back in the cooler.

"That strap won't keep the cooler safely closed," the clerk said, tossing me a heavy roll of clear tape. "Tape it shut."

Oh, if only I could wish him the same!

Then he watched, with great amusement, as I dropped to my knees, balanced the cooler on one shoulder, stretching the tape over, around and under the cooler multiple times, practically prostrate on the floor, flailing and grunting.

With the cooler wrapped like a mummy, I had no tool to cut the tape roll off. The stony-faced airport worker offered nothing, and we all know you can't travel with so much as a nail file anymore. Desperate, this crouching tiger in the downward doggie position chewed the tape free. I'm sure the story made that night's TSA happy hour.

But I'm pleased to report that the filets made it home to the freezer just fine. We've had a fish fry. My sunburn is healing. I'm secretly pleased with my deep-sea adventure. But when we run out of our personal catch, our local Fresh Market seafood department will suffice.

July 2015

NOT JUST ANY FRIDAY!

Well, I had already written my column for this issue and sent it to my editor. The topic was the upcoming marriage equality opinion from the Supreme Court. I was hopeful but not certain. And I expected to add a short addendum to the column at press time, with whatever the news turned out to be.

Hah! *WE WON!!! Holy heck!!!* Unexpected??? I don't know. Great??? *You bet!!!*

I just ripped up that original column with its hedging, guarded hopes. The Supremes, at least five of them, handed us a victory. I wish all of you readers could have been at the CAMP Rehoboth Community Center for the reveal. This was *our* reality show.

A group of us stood around Mark Purpura's laptop computer; you may know, or know of, Mark. He is the crackerjack attorney who wrote the marvelous marriage equality bill for the state of Delaware. We stared at the small screen.

We all suspected this would be the morning for the decision, coming on the anniversary of the earlier Edie Windsor decision. That decision brought marriage equality to states with civil union legislation. This one could bring marriage equality to all 50 states.

Mark stared at his laptop, said. "Here it is," and started to read aloud, then bingo, he stopped in his tracks, looked up and said, quietly, "We won."

For a minute there was no sound in the room. We just stared at Mark and his computer in stunned silence. Then came the whoops, high fives, cheers, and more. "So somebody get the champagne," said a lone voice. It was, after all, 10:05 a.m. Why not?!

Frankly, what happened next was kind of weird. Executive Director Steve and Board President Murray wandered around between the front office and the Community Center room, while we all stared at our cell phones, with more info coming in from posts. There was no radio or TV at CAMP since the streaming signal was weak. In fact, it was oddly quiet for such a joyous moment.

It was as if time were suspended and, after gallons of ink championing marriage equality, hours of testimony, years of marches, decades of disappointments and discrimination, we were just stunned into silence by this enormous victory.

"I can't believe it!"

"I never thought I'd see this in my lifetime."

"For pity's sake somebody put some disco music on!"

And we did. And people started filtering in. We posed for pictures on the CAMP porch, amid balloons and bunting, and thumbs up and smiles a mile wide. Cars passed by and honked, gay folks swarmed the street, straight folks cheered us and blew kisses. It was a true *holy crap* moment.

Finally we got a TV signal and watched President Obama's moving statement. Plans were made for later that afternoon or happy hour or weekend celebrations. I sat down a minute and thought this through. My birthday is three days away. What a birthday present. And although I will be older than dirt on this coming Monday, it amazes me that we are at this juncture at all in my lifetime.

For half my current years (67 if you are counting) it seemed an outright joke and impossibility. At 33 (and a half), I was about to meet my future wife, although there was no hope of using the word wife in any context except for a laugh. We were still sneaking into dingy gay bars in terrible neighborhoods and making up fake boyfriends for work colleagues. (Okay, I never really did that, but I wasn't honest, either.)

At three-quarters of my current lifetime, age 50 or so, we were out and proud and marching and being activists, but marriage equality wasn't even on the table. It still seemed the impossible dream, as simple anti-discrimination bills were failing to gain headway.

One year later, by the way, I moved to Rehoboth full-time, and was able to enjoy the freedom of our gay friendly bubble here on the coast. But we still had absolutely no legal protections or hospital visitation rights, much less any glimmer of potential marriage equality.

As the issue started to snowball in the last (if you are still doing math here) 17 years, Delaware provided hard-fought anti-discrimination protection, then the antiseptic-sounding civil union law, then, gloriously, the full enchilada of marriage equality. Delaware? We were thrilled and pretty darn surprised.

The hard work by our Governor Jack Markell, our local representatives, Equality Delaware and so many more, made the seemingly impossible a reality for our state. And now, here we are, with countrywide marriage rights.

It's fabulous news; it makes a huge difference in many lives and seems the ultimate victory for my 30 years of wishing, hoping, marching, writing, and talking. Fantastic as it is, we all must remember that four Supreme Court judges and an awful lot of Americans think this was a terribly wrong decision.

Implementation may not be smooth. Will we need National Guard troops to ensure marriages can take place in certain states? Will there be violence? What about repercussions? I hope not. But we must be prepared to face whatever comes our way as we see the new law of the land implemented.

There's still work to do. But we can leave that for later! Today, tonight, this last Pride weekend of the month is time to celebrate. I'm heading directly to my favorite watering hole to lift a toast to the fabulous five: Justice Ruth Bader Ginsburg, Justice Anthony M. Kennedy, Justice Sonia Sotomayor, Justice Stephen G. Breyer, and Justice Elena Kagan. You are my heroes.

Oh, and let's not forget Edie Windsor, the courageous woman my dog Windsor is named after, who brought the first marriage equality lawsuit to the Supreme Court and won—that ruling made marriage equality the law of the land in states that had already approved civil unions and gay marriage. Now we can add the name James Obergefell to the hero list, as he is the victor in this current Supreme Court ruling making marriage equality the law of the land in every state in the union.

Gee, good thing we got the dog back in 2014 and named him for Edie. If we had waited until now, his name might have been Obergefell. Try that at the dog park.

And happy birthday to me. Best gift ever.

July 2015

As you know, I absolutely love kayaking except for those two aforementioned things: getting in and getting out.

It continues to be a problem. Not that it deters me, as you've read.

So, a couple of weeks ago it was a brand-new adventure. I accompanied two friends on a kayak ride on Delaware Bay. The rental boats awaited us off a dock, two feet below in the water. It took a platoon of people to hold the kayak up against the pier while I fell into it. "UBE" . . . ugly but effective.

We paddled up the canal, a gentle breeze blowing atop glassy, waveless water. Lovely. Perfect. Easy. I did notice that only one side of my kayak paddle had that little rubber gasket ring above the blade to keep water from dripping down on me. With each stroke, water cascaded directly into Trafalgar Square. It was like throwing cold water on an idea I wasn't even having.

As we traveled the canal and waved at other boaters, one jerk on a personal watercraft came flying by, ignoring the No Wake sign and we were almost swamped. I wouldn't have been surprised to see a small crab in the bottom of my boat.

The sun dried us off as we enjoyed the scenery, then stopped for lunch. We'd decided not to dine at a waterside restaurant as low tide docking would require ejecting myself from the kayak butt hole and hiring a crane to raise me the six feet up to the pier. So, to avoid all that and the headlines it might have produced, we packed peanut butter and jelly. I ate, one hand clutching the sandwich and the other arm hugging an adjacent wooden piling so I wouldn't float off toward Philadelphia.

It was after lunch the real trouble started. As we rounded the mouth of the canal into Delaware Bay, the wind and waves cranked up. Paddling harder but making less forward progress, we could see our final beach destination in the distance. It was supposed to take about an hour to get there.

We paddled mightily, barely making headway. Pretty soon I started to hear loud grunts on each downstroke, making me think Monica Seles was sneaking up behind me. I was astounded to discover the grunter was me. And the soundtrack didn't even help me get ahead.

As I stared at the shore, it was clear that the same brown-shingled cottage, with the same wafting rainbow flag, was staying constant in my field of vision no matter how furiously I paddled. No headway at all.

Like the *Last of the Mohicans*, we paddled our boats with gusto, staying in place, or worse, when we stopped for a breath, going backward. Eventually, we crept forward enough to see different scenery. I think we were in front of the next property for forty minutes, paddling and cursing. Finally, the wind died down a bit and we could inch along towards our beach destination. My arms felt like a rubber Gumby, my ass was asleep, and I was sitting in so much dripped water it was a complimentary sitz bath.

Our simple one-hour kayak trip became the quintessential three-hour tour. If I felt like Ginger or Mary Ann when I started, by the time I hit the beach I was Thurston Howell III. At his wake. So much for a restful day on the water.

But I have to admit, despite the stress I enjoyed it. It's one of the very few things, perhaps the only thing, classified as a sport where I can participate. As my pals hauled me out of my kayak, I staggered up the beach to the parking lot and wondered how I could go about inventing some kind of spring-loaded seat cushion to, as Joe Cocker sang, "lift me up where I belong."

And into the cocktail lounge adjacent to the pier. If golf has its Nineteenth Hole, shouldn't paddling have its Next Wave? I may be onto something delicious . . .

July 2015

Readers know I love New Orleans. Well, we just got back from four weird days there, where Murphy's Law ran amok. It was still a blast, mind you, but it had its challenges.

First, as we flew toward Louisiana, I read a Facebook post from friends down there. Upstream runoff from the great Mississippi River was cascading downstream at an alarming rate. Folks worried that the river would crest over flood stage—and you know what a mess that can be in New Orleans.

On our landing approach, we flew low over some of the canals, and I strained to see if the levees looked stressed. I was stressed, but the levees looked fine. It turned out that while we were in our airport cab, the river crested four inches below panic stage and we could move on to the next crisis.

Arriving at our hotel in 97-degree weather (they give the lesbian conferences July in Louisiana) there was nothing we wanted more than a tall icy cocktail, probably a signature Hurricane. Stopping by our room to unload luggage we were greeted by an urgent hotel advisory: The Sewerage and Water Board issued a Boil Water Order. A power outage at the water plant rendered the entire NOLA water supply unsafe for drinking, tooth-brushing, and showering. *Even showering?*

While I wanted a shower, and would have liked to brush my teeth, the real significance of this meant *no ice.* Here I was in the city where walking around with a Hurricane or other such cocktail was practically mandatory, and there would be no ice. In effect, it became a Boil Water and Drink Beer Order.

So we did, enjoying our red beans and rice, gumbo, oysters, and other celebratory New Orleans menu items. The restaurants were all frustrated, as there could be no sodas, and pretty much no alcoholic drinks served at all, unless you wanted your Scotch neat. Vodka neat is not a thing.

But frankly, after hoofing it around the French Quarter in the excruciatingly hot and humid weather, it was the shower that became mandatory. But, according to the local news, the consequences could be infection with a parasitic brain-eating amoeba—scientific name, *Naegleria fowleri*. It sounded very "fouleri," all right.

So the hotel provided each room with bottled water for drinking, tooth-brushing, and dabbing one's body. *Grand.*

That night I performed my reading in the ballroom at the hotel before a large audience of sweaty lesbians.

Talk about the great unwashed. I might as well have been performing in the woods at the Michigan Womyns Music Festival. I joked that the show title should have been changed from *50 Shades of Fay* to *50 Whiffs of Fay*.

But we survived. I got a standing ovation, although the crowd might just have been standing to air themselves out. Then we all went and had more beer.

The writer's conference itself was magical. Our keynote speaker was Dorothy Allison, author of *Bastard out of Carolina* and other amazing books. Her riveting speech had tales of surviving and thriving at the very dawn of the feminist revolution—and what we, as women, lesbian women specifically, faced and continue to face by way of roadblocks and challenges.

For me, the thrill was sitting next to Ms. Allison at dinner the night before. She was as funny and insightful over shrimp and grits as she was talking to the throngs.

And as if that wasn't enough (and it would have been!) the conference bestowed the Lee Lynch Classic Book Award on pioneering author Rita Mae Brown for her classic *Rubyfruit Jungle*. At the awards ceremony Rita Mae gave a fiery and inspiring speech, imploring us never to be victims and always to remember our roots.

Several years ago, I interviewed her for *Letters* when she was on a book tour with one of her Sneaky Pie mysteries. I got the impression at that time she was all about fox hunting and literary cat stories, no longer so much about activism and LGBT rights. Well, cats and foxes may have been on her mind then, but she's certainly come back home to celebrate her own roots in the feminist revolution and push, push, push for equality. She rocked the ballroom with her words and bravura.

On Sunday morning, before leaving for the airport, Bonnie and I walked along the river toward Café du Monde for beignets and coffee. Just at our left turn into town we heard a deafening train whistle. Who knew that freight trains actually ran through the French Quarter? But there we were, on the wrong side of the tracks from the beignets, watching a lumbering parade of tanker cars, grain carriers and long railroad containers inch by. So slowly in fact, that it took a full 20 minutes, with us baking in the blazing sun, waiting for that insanely long train to pass. Standing just inches from the track, with no gates or barriers, I could have put a bandana on a stick and hopped a boxcar. With only bottled water to sprinkle on the important places, I might have already smelled like a hobo.

And finally, back at the airport, as our plane prepared for take-off, one of its engines quit. The captain apologized and announced they would try to restart the engine. They failed. Again the captain got on the microphone and announced that a ground crew of mechanics was on the way to restart the engine another way. What were they going to do, jump it? I wasn't sure I wanted it to start.

But jump it they did, and off we flew to Baltimore, bidding a fond farewell to brain-eating amoeba, unwashed lesbians, thrilling speakers, tasty gumbo, and my chance to hop a boxcar and become a homo hobo. Despite the challenges it was a fantastic trip. Hey, Rita Mae, we did not choose to be victims!

WARNING! WARNING!

I woke up in the middle of the night with something tickling my mouth and nose, and the bad news was it was neither my spouse nor my dog. It was the tag attached to my new Tempur-Pedic pillow. In a fit of semi-consciousness I ripped the tag off and went back to sleep.

I awoke in the morning to see the tag on my nightstand, saying in large, threatening type, "Do not remove under penalty of law." It wasn't until I thrashed around for my glasses that I could see in teeny type, "except by the consumer."

By nature, I'm a compliant sort. So frankly, while I never thought much about pillow and mattress tags warning me not to remove them, I never removed them, either. I'm sure that in the back of my mind I thought an arrest was possible for felony tag removal.

So I researched this. I am happy to report that even though I've defaced a throw pillow or two in my day, I was never in danger of waking up with Mariska Hargitay in my face (although I would have liked that). But now I was curious who the warning was meant to warn. It seemed so urgent.

As I guessed, but was never certain, the warning is not for those of us sleeping with these pillows and mattresses and routinely having to spit out crinkly tags. They are for the pillow and mattress sellers only. Continuing my research, I discovered that the purpose is to inform the consumer of the hidden filler materials inside bedding and furniture.

The law mandating the tags goes back to the early 1900s, to prevent pillows and such from being manufactured with specious contents such as horsehair, cornhusks, garbanzo beans, or worse. Because nobody wants to snuggle with cornhusks.

But I believe that for years, people have been confused by these labels, because the wording "except by the consumer" was not added until many decades after the labels appeared. Also, as we know, people don't often bother to read stuff (hoping this column is an exception).

Indeed, it made me think about why I dislike labels. Not in the fashionable sense of disliking the labels representing LGBTQ or whatever other alphabet letter is next to get annexed, but labels in general.

Just coincidentally, later that same morning, I got on a ladder in my shed to reach some old tax returns.

Holy cow. There were more warning labels on that ladder than bumper stickers on a 1970 Volkswagen bus. Have you seen a ladder lately? I can only imagine the litigation that prompted one six-foot ladder to sport the following labels, some with little stick figure illustrations:

• CAUTION: KEEP BODY CENTERED BETWEEN SIDE RAILS. There was a stick figure leaning in a position my body, never mind a contortionist's, will never go.

• DO NOT OVER-REACH. I don't even know what this means, unless it's talking about me over-reaching for a pun or something.

• DO NOT CLIMB, STAND OR SIT ABOVE SECOND STEP FROM TOP. Are the top steps just decorative?

• MAKE SURE LADDER IS FULLY OPEN AND SPREADERS LOCKED. I'm speechless. Or, to be literal, type-less.

• SET ALL FEET ON FIRM, LEVEL SURFACE. My feet or the ladder's? My feet are so ugly, the drawing could apply to both.

• DO NOT PLACE IN FRONT OF UNLOCKED DOORS. I can see the lawsuit that prompted this warning. "Honey, I'm home! Um . . . hello, 9-1-1?"

• FACE LADDER WHEN CLIMBING, USE BOTH HANDS AND DO NOT CARRY OBJECTS IN YOUR HANDS. So much for me climbing up with a Cosmo in one hand and paintbrush in the other. But how would you get the paint can to the top of the ladder without your hands? Helicopter?

• GET DOWN AND MOVE LADDER AS NEEDED. Is there an alternative? The Think System?

• DO NOT SIT ATOP AND STRADDLE FRONT AND BACK. It is not a horse.

• DO NOT CLIMB FROM ONE LADDER TO ANOTHER. Unless your name is Wallenda.

• DO NOT SHIFT LADDER WHILE ON IT. You mean like into second gear?

• NEVER PLACE LADDER ON OTHER OBJECTS SUCH AS BOXES, SCAFFOLDS OR OTHER UNSTABLE BASES TO OBTAIN ADDITIONAL HEIGHT. My imagination runs away . . .

Seriously, I spent at least an hour marveling at the incredible amount of labeling on a single ladder and it distracted me nicely from my task. When I did get the paperwork down, I took it directly to my office for shredding. OMG. The warning labels on the shredder were just as bad! They were all little graphics with the international "NO" sign on it—the circle with a slash through it. I think they meant:

• Do not dangle long hair or spaghetti in shredder.

• Don't ever wear a tie.

• No manicures or if the glove doesn't fit you must acquit.

It's enough to make me give up my tasks and take a nap. But first, under penalty of law, I'll rip the remaining labels off my pillows. See you on *Orange Is the New Black*.

August 2015

This is your roving reporter writing from a bench in the Athens airport, 11 a.m. Greek time.

Luckily, I signed onto the hotel Wi-Fi last night to find a message from my editor. "Will you be back in time to send me a column by deadline?"

Um, no. But where there's a Wi-Fi there's a way. So here I sit, typing with my thumbs on my smartphone. Our Greek Islands Olivia Cruise, starting in Istanbul, was so joyously fascinating, mere adjectives are not enough. Great job, Olivia!

Did you know that part of Istanbul is in Asia and part in Europe? News to me. Imagine commuting between continents for work. In Istanbul we loved the spice market and mosques. The city is very progressive, and while we saw more than a few women covered in burkas or in black robes with just their faces showing, we learned they were mostly tourists from Saudi Arabia, etc. Burkas are outlawed in Istanbul.

We were only there a day, after nearly 24 hours of travel, so we drank ridiculously strong Turkish coffee to stay awake long enough to buy Turkish spices at the market. We even bought Iranian saffron, patently illegal to purchase at home. And we covered our arms and heads to visit the beautiful Blue Mosque.

Since this was an all-lesbian cruise, first stop was the Isle of Lesbos, only it's called Lesvos because apparently Lesvosians cannot pronounce the letter *B*. Who knew? Or perhaps they want to distance themselves from their Sapphic sisters, which is entirely possible.

Upon hearing our itinerary, a straight friend asked if we lesbians were expected to make a pilgrimage to the island once in our lifetime, like a hajj to Mecca or a crawl on the knees to Fatima. No, I said, I didn't think so. And that's a good thing, as the island had not so much to recommend it. At least where we toured. In fact, our Olivia gang seemed to be the only discernible examples of the island's namesakes around.

Among the hundreds of trinkets and souvenirs for sale, almost nothing spoke of dear Sappho, although I managed to snag a coffee cup with her supposed likeness on it. Our guide celebrated Sappho for her poetry, school for women, and message that women could learn, write, and be leaders! Tell that to the GOP. We drank 48 proof Ouzo, which tasted like liquid Good and Plenty, and toasted to Sappho.

There was a surprising and sadly newsworthy sight in Lesvos—newly arrived Syrian refugees, many of them with tents and camping supplies, bedding down all over the island. I can say this for the Lesbosians: They are a welcoming lot, assisting the refugees at every turn.

Okay, our flight is boarding for the homeland . . . I'll be back to you shortly!

So now it is three hours later, and we are flying over France. Eight hours to go before we land in Toronto. My thumbs got a rest from typing, so here I go again, refreshed . . .

On the cruise to the Greek Isles, each stop we visited was more magnificent than the last. In Ephesus (back in Turkey again) we toured 2,500-year-old ruins—lots of old rocks and busted pottery, painstakingly reassembled like a five-million-piece jigsaw puzzle. Astounding! I could envision the chariots racing and Antony and Cleo strolling around. Only one quarter of the site has been excavated, and I hope I get back someday to see more.

Next came Crete with its beautiful harbor, exquisite jewelry, terrific souvlaki, and . . . here's the best part: fish spas! It's a big thing in Crete. We dangled our feet in fish tanks so our toes and heels could be nibbled into softness. When I first dipped my toes into the water, the nibbling fish tickled so much I screamed, then almost passed out from laughing. This is a huge business in Crete. I'm thinking of opening a fish spa on Rehoboth Avenue. I would prefer to manage a spa rather than get nibbled, thank you.

Next up, Santorini. When you see pictures of the Greek Isles, it's Santorini you see—cities atop a volcanic mountain, all-white structures with blue domes. Stunning.

Once on shore, we had two choices to get up to the mountain-top town: a clean, safe cable car, or by riding a dirty, smelly donkey up the steep, narrow, frightening path. Now you know I'll do almost anything for a good story, but while the scary topography and danger did not worry me, it was the donkey aroma that put me in the cable car. Sorry.

Once in the city, we walked upward for over an hour, on stone paths and steps, through the picturesque town of Fira, continuing until our knees completely gave out. I believe that Santorini tourism is funded solely by orthopedic surgeons.

In self-defense, we rented a tiny dune buggy and crammed our big butts into it, continuing the climb with Bonnie driving like a madwoman, dodging tour buses and scooters on skinny, cliff-side roads. Fabulous, death-defying, fun. I probably should have ridden that malodorous donkey to make the day complete.

Time out. Gotta nap.

Oh good god, we just touched down in Toronto, 14 hours since we left the hotel in Athens. Now we have four hours until liftoff to Newark. My ankles are swollen like beach balls, I need emergency chiropractic, and we are just now heading for customs. I'll be back to you after I get sniffed by dogs. Hopefully I smell better than a Santorini donkey, but I cannot promise.

Okay, back on the plane again. That was an ordeal. After customs, where I avoided mentioning the Iranian saffron in my suitcase, we had to go through security for the second time today. Standing barefoot, watching my possessions go into the dark maw of the x-ray machine, I silently cursed that stupid underpants bomber who started all this.

So we're back in the air, heading for New Jersey now, thumbs flying as well on my tiny iPhone keyboard. The last island we visited was Mykonos—of gorgeous beaches, stunning views, and hot nightlife. We loved it. For anyone who knows the play or film *Shirley Valentine*, I got to sit just where the movie was filmed!

Unfortunately we had to leave the island before the clubs opened. But our day at the beach was marvelous.

Then it was off the ship in Athens to visit the Acropolis—the enormous hill that's the highest point in the city, and the Parthenon—the amazingly reconstructed, columned edifice perched atop the giant rock. Up close and personal it was awesome and mind-bogglingly ancient. Several blocks away, from our dinner table on the rooftop of the hotel, it was an unbelievably beautiful sight.

Fasten your seatbelts and put your tray tables in an upright position. Welcome to New Jersey. We're at the hotel, collapsing before the drive home to the beach tomorrow. We've been traveling without sleep for just about 24 hours now. It's been a memorable week, surrounded by feta cheese, antiquities, and 600 lesvians. Oh how I loved it. Over and out, sweet readers.

August 2015
EASY RIDER, OR LOOK MA, NO HANDS!

My new bike was delivered yesterday.

That I bought one at all is odd, as I have a very speckled history when it comes to biking. I didn't learn to ride a bike until I was 32. I still see my adult self, wobbling down the street with a cadre of other adults running behind me yelling "You can do it, you can do it!" It was right out of the film *Kramer vs. Kramer*, only in that case Dustin Hoffman cheered on a six-year-old.

Quite pathetically, I had forced myself to learn to ride a bicycle to impress a new love in my life. My novice biking status unshared, my amour and I took a total of two 'round the block rides and one jaunt on the very flat Eastern Shore of Maryland before I made a tactical error.

Still in the glow of this new relationship, I agreed to take a vacation where we'd abandon the car on Cape Cod and take our bikes and backpacks on a ferry to Nantucket.

I did this despite never once feeling stable on two wheels and, in fact, certain I had an inner ear disorder preventing me from staying upright. That I'm a math moron and could balance a checkbook better than balance my butt on a bike scared me. Further frightening me was my riding style. Not once while previously pedaling did I ever look at any scenery, staring instead the entire time at my front tire and praying I would not wipe out.

So this liar, liar handlebars on fire went on the bike adventure anyway. I have to say, I felt uncharacteristically sporty and even a bit smug standing with my bike on the ferry, luggage hanging from my back. I loved thinking that the auto passengers saw me as somebody who would take this kind of excursion.

My self-righteousness was short-lived. We docked at a cobblestone ramp, followed by an even bumpier cobblestone street. It was, literally, a rocky start. And our hotel was four blocks straight up a steep hill. I attempted to ride, but after two grunting false starts, a close call at T-boning a parked car and almost taking out a family of four, I wound up walking my Schwinn up the entire ghastly hill.

We finally arrived at the Lucretia Mott House Hotel, named for an American women's rights activist and social reformer. Noticing my considerable distress at schlepping the Schwinn—perhaps it was the wheezing—my companion said, "Let's lock the bikes up and go get a drink."

Clearly disgusted, I replied, "Let's *not* lock the bikes up and hope mine gets stolen."

Things were not going well. But at least the Mott House had a handy cocktail lounge. Lucretia may have had many social causes, but I'm guessing that the temperance movement wasn't among them. So the bikes were locked and we got loaded.

The next morning, we bounced our bikes down the cobblestone grade and set out on a nice, flat, paved road to the ocean. With a stiff wind at our backs, we got quite a push in the pedaling department, making it an easy and unexpectedly comfortable ride. I even looked up from my front tire occasionally to admire the historic homes, rooftop widow's walks, and spectacular landscaping. We'd ridden three miles in fifteen minutes without incident. I'm not saying I was doing wheelies, but at least I remained vertical.

At water's edge, the wind continued to whip as we took obligatory photos and enjoyed the sights and sounds of surf and seagulls.

But then it was time to go back to town. The wind, which provided such a lovely lift on the way to the shore, was now squarely in our faces, holding us back, making each straining turn of the pedals a year of hard labor. With aching legs and burning lungs, we saw happy bikers coming at us, giggling and zipping toward the beach. "Laugh now, you idiots!" I hollered, "Because you'll never get back!!!"

As I pedaled, panted, and wobbled, turkey buzzards circled overhead, tagging me for future roadkill. At one point I squeezed my brakes, hopped off the bike, emitted a string of expletives, and threw the vehicle down. But the sorry sight of my companion trying to wrangle a bike in each hand got me back in the saddle.

It was an hour's struggle. I'd taken one ugly spill, skinned both knees, and twisted my ankle on my dismount in Lucretia Mott's parking lot. An ice bag and several Band-Aids later, we went to dinner, having negotiated a pact to spend the rest of the vacation on foot.

I am happy to report that despite my false advertising as a Tour de France contestant and my less than sterling behavior in Nantucket, the relationship flourished. We've been together thirty-three years now, thirty-two years, eight months since that unfortunate cycling expedition.

I never rode that bike again, and in fact, it was last seen rusted to the garage wall, conveyed to the home's new owners when we moved to Rehoboth 15 years ago.

So why in heck did I just get a brand-new Schwinn? And why did my spouse happily return from K-Mart with handlebar streamers, a horn, and a deck of cards to put in the wheel spokes?

Because my new Schwinn has three wheels. I've named her Lucretia.

September 2015

I've written about this before, but I had a compelling experience last weekend, and I want to share.

I performed my reading *Aging Gracelessly* before a mostly straight audience in Annapolis. While the performance was a success, with lots of laughs and much appreciation, it was very, very different than doing the show with a mostly gay audience here in Rehoboth.

For instance, when, performing for our crowd, I said, "Back in the early '80s, when I read up on homosexuality, the news wasn't so good. I thought I'd have to learn to play softball," our gay gang laughed like hell. In Annapolis, the six lesbians and four gay men in the house laughed and snorted, but that was pretty much it.

Yes, it's a cultural thing. Straight folks had no touchstone about mid-20th century lesbians naturally finding each other on softball teams. At another point, I realized I should skip the lesbians and the U-Haul joke.

The night brought home to me that gay is a culture all its own, and we may be in danger of losing it. With all of our forward strides in equality and assimilation into the mainstream community at large, I think we have to work hard to keep our culture from disappearing altogether.

Recently there was an online flap about the trailer for the new film *Stonewall* about the 1969 uprising in Greenwich Village, NYC. I'm glad there are folks still around to take exception to the preview showing predominantly gay white men front and center. In fact, it was transgender Latinos and black drag queens, along with some butch lesbians front and center, as well as the gay white guys.

The first people in the paddy wagon at the start of the riots were the feisty Latino transwomen. The producers of the film recognized that the trailer upset folks and promised that the film is actually accurate.

We shall see.

But in the meantime, does anybody remember the name of one of those heroic drag queens? We should. For the record it was Silvia Rivera, who passed away recently. She was central to the story, along with other drag queens as well as many of the middle-class, white gay men at the bar.

But the truth is, our gay culture has a lot of pioneering activists and celebrity performers whose names and stories have been central to our history—and whose names today mean nothing to many, many folks in our community. And that's a shame.

I think we owe it to ourselves to pass along gay history and culture to our succeeding generations. After all, unless they are lesbians or gay men, the parents of our younger generations are not going to pass this culture on to their children. It's got to be our job. Here's a test. Billy Joel's song "We Didn't Start the Fire"—with new words. How many references do you know?

Harvey Milk, Harry Hay, Laramie, Come Out Day
San Francisco, Bayard Rustin, tiny church named Westboro
Larry Kramer, Phyllis Lyon, Stonewall Inn, brothers dying
Northampton, Provincetown, Rehomo and men in gowns
HRC, Barney Frank, Rita Mae, we all drank
Liberace, Cleve Jones, Pride parades and macho clones
Bar'bra Gittings, silver screen, England's own Elton queen
Matthew Shepard, MCC, Ask, Tell and Kameny
Katherine Forrest, Naiad Press, Quentin Crisp was a mess
Truman C, Danny Kaye, yelling "Queer!" is not okay|
They helped to start the fire
The streets were raging
And the world was changing
They helped to start the fire . . .

How'd you do? Do you know the names Troy Perry or Paul Lynde? How about film director George Cukor? Perry Mason himself, Raymond Burr? A-plus if you do. If not, we need to spread our history around some more.

I have a friend who loves classic movies with a gay sensibility or story—such as *The Women, All About Eve, The Children's Hour.* He invites gay friends who don't know the films over for a Gay 101 night. I love the idea.

If I had Lesbian 101 at my house I'd start with *The Killing of Sister George, The Fox, Desert Hearts,* and *Tipping the Velvet.* That sounds like such fun I think I'll do it. And while I'm at it I'll casually ask if anyone knows who Del Martin was, or Mary Martin, for that matter, or if they've ever heard of the Daughters of Bilitis. Or Mrs. Danvers?

How about Katharine Hepburn and her housekeeper, or Eleanor Roosevelt and journalist Lorena Hickok? Or Agnes Moorehead on *Bewitched?* Now there's real culture for you. We'll have wine, we'll discuss women and song and a whole lot more. Pass it on.

September 2015

People talk about traffic and gridlock at my beach resort as if our Route One is New York's 42nd Street. They complain that you could gestate a baby there on Sunday afternoons. That nobody dares go "out on the highway" on Saturday from 11 to noon. That we should all age in place Fridays 5-9 p.m. and Sundays 4-7. Well I'm here to tell you, our traffic can't hold a candle to the real 42nd Street.

I've just been a part of it, New York, New York.

And while I'm a Big Apple native, I have not lived there for over 40 years. I did, however, think I'd still be king of the hill and top of the heap with my big city driving and honking skills. No way.

I spent an entire hour circling midtown Manhattan at up to 13 mph, dodging trucks, Uber limos, taxis, pedestrians, racks of clothes in the garment district, bike messengers, and dog walkers, as we tried to get to a specific garage where I had prepaid for parking.

Apparently, since I last trolled the city that never sleeps, the mayor added NO LEFT TURN signs at every intersection, except for the ones with NO RIGHT TURN signs. The streets are mostly one way so you have to cross the entire Isle of Manhattan before they let you turn, lest you wind up in the East River.

On our second cross-town tour, when we turned off Park Avenue toward 43rd Street, we got caught up in the maze of roads going right through the very heart of it, New York, New York's Grand Central Station building. We traveled in a dizzying circle, only to be spit out facing uptown.

Following an illegal U-turn, (But officer, we're from Delawhere??) we inched back down this gridlocked island purchased in 1620 by the Dutch from Native Americans for 24 bucks. We spent at least that in gasoline looking for our stupid discount garage.

And for much of the hour, there was an ice cream van up ahead playing shrill calliope music, although it was way too late for us to have lost our minds to that. We crossed through Times Square so often Madame Tussaud should have put us in her Wax Museum; we saw the same homeless man twice, both times talking on his iPhone; we crept so slowly I could jump out for a street vendor pretzel without running to catch up.

In Times Square, people crossed our path dressed like giant M&Ms, Minions, and the Statue of Liberty. You could buy bad art, Prada knockoffs, and a phony Movado wristwatch by just reaching out your car window. I saw a naked cowboy and two women with their breasts covered only by body-painted American flags. I'd say they stopped traffic but it was already stopped.

At long last, when a legitimate, allowable right turn was in sight, our glee was dashed by a honking fire engine coming from behind and forcing us to the left side of the street. In our quest for the so near and yet so far West 43rd street, we had to make a brand-new start of it, in old New York.

One driver took the law into his hands, stopped by a parking space with a bright orange cone blocking it, removed the cone, parked, and stashed the cone on the roof of his car. People in traffic applauded.

Flowing masses of pedestrians crossed in front of, behind, and alongside cars. If it would have helped, they'd have opened rear car doors, scooted across back seats, and hopped out the other side. People alternately carried and protected themselves with briefcases, trash bags, luggage, and pizza boxes; people pushed walkers, strollers, vendor carts, and each other; a young woman crossed by our hood ornament in a skirt so short you could see up to Madison Square Garden.

From high fashion to low life, people wore business suits, short-shorts, jogging gear, designer dresses, pajamas, and rags. There were yarmulkes, headscarves, ear buds, and Yankee caps. It was 91 degrees out. Everybody's little town blues were literally melting away.

Finally, a full 55 minutes since we started this round robin, we hollered "Uncle," forfeited our prepaid parking, and pulled into the nearest parking garage.

We saw a new Broadway musical called *Something Rotten*. It was hilarious. But clearly, the title referred to our excruciating pre-show traffic challenge.

Just so you know, I have officially renounced my Big Apple driver's license. If I'm in New York, New York it will be Uber or Yellow cab from now on. The convenience of a roadside Nathan's hot dog stand or a grab-n-go New York cheesecake slice aside, these particular vagabond shoes are longing to stray back to Delaware.

Start spreading the news.

October 2015

You probably think the headline above is about my dog Windsor, but you would be wrong. It's about me. I have learned to bark.

I was in Provincetown, Massachusetts, on Cape Cod last week for Women's Week, signing books and doing my *Aging Gracelessly* show. And, as I knew, all performers in P-town follow a somewhat degrading, but ultimately beneficial tradition of barking.

The performers walk up and down Commercial Street, handing out postcards advertising their upcoming shows, shamelessly self-promoting to unsuspecting and often uninterested or occasionally hostile pedestrians. It's a throwback to the long-held American tradition of circus barking, as in standing in front of the circus tent, encouraging patrons to come inside.

The streets of P-town are filled with barkers—comics Jennie McNulty, Poppy Champlin, and Karen Williams do it; the comedy troupe The Dykes of Hazard did it; drag kings and queens do it; rich and famous entertainers hire other people to do it for them.

According to Wikipedia, "a barker is a person who attempts to attract patrons to entertainment events . . . by exhorting passing public, describing the show . . . to incite listeners to attend entertainment." Barkers are also called touts, described as "any person who solicits business in a persistent and annoying manner." Oh fun.

And the information you pass along as you bark in an annoying manner is your spiel. Although in my culture we pronounce it schpeel, as in "stop with the schpeel already and hand me a bagel."

I arrived in P-town on Tuesday afternoon, and my show was set for Wednesday night, so I needed to get barking and "exhorting the passing public" in a hurry. After all, there were at least five comics and many more musicians with shows at the exact same time as mine on Wednesday. The only saving grace was that Kate Clinton, Poppy, Jennie, Suzanne Westenhoefer, Vickie Shaw, and the others had shows every night, and I was only doing mine once—so thankfully, if folks took time to come and see my show, they still had lots of opportunities to check out the real lesbian celebrity comics, or celesbians as I like to call them.

After watching celesbians Jennie and Poppy chat confidently with passersby (they had great spiels) and hand out postcards about their shows, I steeled myself and hit the streets to pimp myself out and give folks my spiel.

Somewhat hesitantly I headed toward a group of women and, postcard in my outstretched hand, tipped said hand, so to speak, and they avoided me like I had cooties. With the next group of gay girls coming down the street I tried the stealth system—saying, "Hi," then springing the postcards on them. They were polite but not particularly enthused.

Next came the apologetic approach. "Hi, I'm a new performer in town, just learning this street-walking thing, won't you take my postcard?" This seemed to elicit some sympathy and piqued their interest. Several women actually looked at my postcard and asked a question or two about the show. Progress.

Ultimately, I combined the apology tactic with the smiling moron methodology, walking along, grinning, and inserting myself into the conversations of strangers. That one was pretty effective, as a couple of women even promised to come to the show.

After about an hour and a half, including a stop for a lobster roll, I gave up and went to Poppy's show, followed by Jennie's performance. They were both awesome, with the audience, me included, screaming with laughter.

Now I was scared. I'm doing a show in P-town??? What have I gotten myself into??? How can I compete with these Queer Queens of Comedy??? Not to mention my idol Kate Clinton. *Oy.*

By the next morning I was in a cold sweat, thinking about all the barking I had yet to do and the performance I was scheduled to give. Was I barking up the wrong tree? Why did I agree to do this silly thing???

I joined my friend, author Lynn Ames, and my author colleagues from Bywater Books (Marianne K. Martin and Georgia Beers) for a book signing at the venerable Womencrafts bookstore. Yes, it's still there after all these years.

My pals got me to relax and chill a little as we met readers and signed some books. From there, it was back to street-walking for me. I girded my loins and launched into the fray, knowing this was my last chance to round up an audience for that night's show. As demeaning as the barking may have been, an empty house would be mortifyingly worse.

But wait! The first couple I saw said, "Hello, Fay!" as they eagerly accepted my postcard. After a lovely conversation, I walked away, buoyed by the fact that they had recognized me. In fact, the next few groups of women easily accepted my intrusion and thrusting of postcards, again, with one of the gals greeting me by name even before reading the ad in her hand. This was way cool!

My head might have started to swell a little as I eagerly traversed the streets and gave out lots of postcards, chatting easily with folks along the way and being really impressed that so many people already knew me. Hey, this was starting to be fun!

It wasn't until I stopped at Spiritus for a slice of pizza that I looked down and realized I was still wearing my "Hello My Name Is Fay" name tag from the book signing. You moron! *They were reading your name, you idiot!!!* So much for fame and name recognition. I had to laugh. But the truth was, once my confidence was up I really had a fun time barking and touting and promoting my show.

As it turned out, the show was a sell-out. Waaay more people showed up than I had expected, and my debut as a P-town performer went well. Poppy had time before her next show to see my first act and Jennie ran over to see my second act when her show let out. I cannot thank them enough for the support. Their complimentary comments meant a lot to me.

And for the rest of the week, since my show was over, any time I got a chance, I happily barked about theirs. Oh, and Kate Clinton's show was absolutely hilarious; Karen Williams cracked us up, too.

So I've had my street-walking trial by fire. I'm honored to be found soliciting on the same street as my comic idols. Like Windsor, this last comic sitting has learned to bark her head off. Woof.

November 2015

It was just a matter of time before somebody introduced me to Trivia Crack.

I used to love the old Trivial Pursuit game. I got my first edition of the game in ... wait for it ... 1981. And I still had that 35-year-old classic edition until last year. One night we got the tattered box out of the closet (reminding me that in 1981 I was practically still *in* the closet) and had a game. Hilarity ensued.

Not only had we players aged gracelessly, but the game aged worse than we did—incredible as that may seem. You see, that old game had questions like, "What's the Soviet Union's political arm called?" (Defunct?) or "When is RFK's assassin Sirhan Sirhan scheduled for parole?" (um, the answer was a chilling 1994, but thankfully he didn't make parole and died before his hearing came up again).

"What woman has won the most Wimbledon championships?" It was Billie Jean King in 1981, but then Martina Navratilova came along!

"British Airways and Air France" was the answer to "What two airlines fly the Concorde to Europe?" By this time the answer was "Nobody, that plane has been scrapped!" The game was seriously showing its age.

One question after another was impossible to answer, not because we were ignorant, but because the facts of life had changed (well, not *those* facts of life, but you know what I mean.) Everything old was not new again, and we consigned the vintage game to the dumpster.

Surprisingly, I had a never-unwrapped, 20th Anniversary Edition of Trivial Pursuit in that aforementioned closet as well. Even that game was old school, since not only had it been 15 years of life, liberty, and a deluge of trivia since the update was introduced, all of the questions were from 1990-2000. Our inability to answer most of them showed us just how fleeting pop culture has become.

Where lots of the original questions asked about history or geography or classic literature, these questions offered up flash-in-the-pan celebrities and song titles that seemed to disappear as completely as the devices we used to play them on. Cassette tapes, anyone?

When we got to the question of "What classic toy celebrated its 50th Anniversary in 2000?" we all realized we were older than Silly Putty. That was sobering.

As we failed to succeed at answering, we figured the names, places, and events hadn't stood the test of time, or else we all dozed through the '90s. Our gang was so horrid at this old new edition it would have been Trivial Pursuit's 50th Anniversary by the time we answered enough questions for somebody to win the game.

But we had our memories! Those original trivia categories, as in Blue for Geography and Pink for Entertainment (universally acknowledged as my best category!), were known so well by us that they became part of our daily conversation.

Over dinner, or at a bar, somebody would ask, "Who was that actor in, you know, um . . ." and several people might answer, "Is that a Pink question?"

I would also like to note that the new board was way flimsier than the old sturdy cardboard one, slightly smaller and with cheesier plastic "pie" pieces. In unison we got to say "They're not making them like they used to!"

There was, however, a new card dispenser to help keep the cards organized and distributed. Although for those of us whose knuckles are more arthritic today than they were in 1980, the thing was a bitch to get going.

So there we were, trying to answer things like, "What 1997 PlayStation game obliged players to teach a cartoon dog to rap and dance well enough to win over his girlfriend?" Seriously? In case you care, the answer nobody knew was PaRappa the Rapper.

Do you know, "What line in *Big Brother* appeared in closed

captioning as 'your colon smells good'?" None of us wanted to know that one, but it turned out it should have said "cologne." Apparently none of us watched *Big Brother* and now we are glad. And both of those questions came from my stellar Pink category Entertainment, or Sound and Screen as it was renamed.

So out went the 20th Anniversary Edition, too, replaced just recently by that invitation for me to play online Trivia Crack. If you've been under the proverbial rock, Trivia Crack is a mobile app that allows users to compete against friends and people around the world.

Modeled after Trivial Pursuit, it was the most downloaded game in 2014, hence the comparison to a disastrously addictive drug. It is insanely addicting. My friend Sparky urged me to play, and I can now say, that yes, I played enough to lose an entire 48 hours in the month of October. I couldn't stop. It was like I was shooting up, glued to my iPhone or computer 24/7. Just one more, just one more, just one more.

But here's the thing. I was just as bad at Trivia Crack as the other trivia games. In fact, after about a day and a half of bleary-eyed Q&A I finally got a Pink question to win my game. Much to my horror my screen lit up with the phrase, "This is your worst category!"

Not only had they been keeping tabs on me, but they were rubbing it in. Here's the deal. Apparently I have not really listened to pop music since my forties; the History category is painful because the questions still seem like current events to me; and my beloved Pink Questions are now about anonymous people who weren't even born when I first rocked out on Pink Questions.

When somebody comes up with the Old Fart Edition of Trivial Pursuit, with answers like Perry Como, Cher, "Yellow Submarine," and "Lipstick on Your Collar," please let me know. And if you are reading this and don't recognize the name Perry Como, please don't let me know.

CAROL IS THE NEW *DESERT HEARTS*

What a difference 30 years makes.

I'm talking about the metamorphosis between the day Bonnie and I saw the 1985 premier of the landmark lesbian movie *Desert Hearts* in Washington, D.C. and a few weeks ago when we saw *Carol*, also a lesbian-themed film, at the local multiplex.

That one of my friends joining us at the movies was also along for the original *Desert Hearts* screening made the comparison that much sweeter. But here's what three decades can do.

I remember the *Desert Hearts* premiere like yesterday (probably better than yesterday, alas), seeing hundreds of women converging on the theater and loitering outside. At that time, except for the 1983 March on Washington, I'd never seen so many lesbians together in public before. Seedy bars in bad neighborhoods, yes, but in plain sight in the nation's capital? Motorists negotiating Washington Circle had never seen such a thing either, leading to, I swear, several screeching tires and at least two fender benders in the half-hour before the theatre doors opened.

But it was inside where history happened. The audience had never before seen themselves represented on screen in a positive light, much less in a love story with a happy ending. Previously, all we saw were the few lesbian stories where one lover had to be thrown under the bus—hit by a falling tree, like Sandy Dennis in *The Fox*, or hanging from the rafters like Shirley MacLaine in *The Children's Hour*.

With *Desert Hearts*, the audience watched, transfixed, as prim Helen Shaver and cute Patricia Charbonneau, a "hottie" in today's vernacular, met, intrigued each other, and had an affair—including a beautiful love scene.

As the women kissed, you could feel the electricity and sexual tension in the theater. At a literally climactic moment, somebody got carried away and squealed, "Oh my!" The rest of the crowd burst out laughing.

I know that every single woman in the theatre that night remembers the film, that endearing outburst, and the historic nature of the evening. Heterosexuals had been watching themselves clasp and gasp on film since *Birth of a Nation*, but this was our very first chance to experience a filmed love story about people like us. It was magic.

Of course, by comparison, *Desert Hearts* was G-rated clasping and gasping. Today, the love scene in *Carol* is as realistic and intimate as any straight love scene filmed these days. And while there was also electricity generated throughout the audience, there was no self-conscious laughter, no feeling of history, certainly no fender benders precipitated by a gaggle of lesbians buying tickets. Although I cannot vouch for current incidents caused by our retirement community's cataracts or slowed reflexes.

Thirty years ago we were still outlaws in most places, fairly recently declared free of mental illness, with most of us at least partially closeted. In Rehoboth, homophobic T-shirts unabashedly hung in store windows, name-calling and even gay bashing was rife, and tomatoes were still being lobbed into our bars. There was an uneasy and suspicious divide between Rehoboth homeowners and visiting gay tourists. CAMP Rehoboth was five years yet from its birth as a nonprofit, and the AIDS epidemic, just starting, made things much worse before they started to get better.

It's ironic—both *Desert Hearts* and *Carol* spotlight really tough times, the 1950s and '60s—for their lesbian characters. *Desert Hearts* came from a 1964 book by Jane Rule and took place in 1960s Reno, Nevada. *Carol* is from a 1952 book by Patricia Highsmith, and highlights the steep price two women pay for choosing to be together. But exactly like *Desert Hearts*, the film has a really (Spoiler Alert!) . . . hopeful ending.

Back in '85 Bonnie and I had no official recognition as a couple. We'd gather with friends in a dangerous part of D.C. at gay bars with no names on the door, a hefty cover to get in, and a creepy, scary walk back to our car later.

Most of our neighbors wouldn't even talk to us; we feared telling employers we were gay, lest they (completely legally) fire us for just that knowledge; we were young and having fun, but it was unwise to be too "out."

It was so rare to see lesbians on film or television that every time we were featured on TV, I'd tape the episode on my Betamax video tape recorder. There was an episode on *Maude* with Bea Arthur, a peck of a kiss on *L.A. Law*, and a charming episode of *The Golden Girls* (again, Bea Arthur. Hmmmm?).

These days you'd get dizzy trying to record (digitally, what's tape?) all the stories, commercials and news reports featuring us.

Now, we're married seniors, jointly filing taxes, living completely out of the closet. Here in Delaware (but not everywhere in the nation—yet) we cannot be fired just for being gay, and I love calling Bonnie my wife.

Is everything perfect? Hell no. There's lots of work still to be done. But we live in a lesbian paradise, can dine and dance comfortably anywhere we want, and in most cases, our only limitations are the ones we put upon ourselves. For some, it's tough to get used to the broken barriers.

And it sure was fun to join the throng of lesbians and others converging at the movies. As far as I could tell, nobody batted an eye at us. Go see *Carol*. It's a terrific film. But it's not a historic experience. And that's a great thing.

March 2016

I AM MY OWN ROADIE

Greetings from *Aging Gracelessly*, the tour.

Yes, I'm having a blast touring with my show and staying well south of the snow. But we're not exactly traveling like the big acts, with a fancy bus and a hoard of advance people. Bonnie and Windsor are crew and we get to schlepp all the props, sound equipment, and related rubbish all by ourselves.

We headed out of Reho in January, SUV jammed with multiple sets of suitcases for various gigs and so much gear, Windsor looked buried alive in his car seat. The Schnauzermobile recalled the *Beverly Hillbillies*, piled high with sound equipment, dog crate, doggie stroller, Bonnie's watercolors, my camera gear, and a set of specifically packed overnight bags—one for the trip down and another for my upcoming Olivia cruise gig, with clothes, scripts, music, microphone, music stand and my giant martini glass. Then we had two large bulging suitcases for the rest of the winter's hibernation.

On our first night out, after a long day on I-95, we stopped in South Carolina for a good night's sleep. At first we were annoyed at blaring music from the room next door. Then we were begrudgingly amused but eventually annoyed at the headboard thumping and other extremely descriptive noises the participants tried to mask with Lady Gaga. *Oy*, what endurance!

Here at the Roadway Inn, I'd say somebody was rode way hard and put away, well, you know.

We were finally all sacked out when the phone rang at 3:30 in the morning.

"Is that your dog barking?" asked the front desk.

"No, that's my dog yawning. You woke him up." Not a good night.

By day two, grumpy and mistrusting our GPS, Bonnie fiddled with said bitch on the dashboard as I consulted my iPhone's GPS function. Later, when I went for a potty break, I was descending to the throne when my pocket announced, "When possible make a U-turn." Laughter ensued from all the stalls.

Finally, we arrived in Ft. Lauderdale, left Windsor with his trusted dog-sitter, and headed for the cruise ship. You may have read my comments about Olivia before. I was a late-adopter, having enjoyed many a "regular" cruise. In fact, I was snarky about it, wondering how an Olivia Cruise, which cost a bit more money, could be so much better to be worth the added cost.

Well, following my first Olivia Cruise in 2008, I admitted my grievous error. It was more than worth it. After this, my third cruise, the issue is settled for me. No matter your age, interests, or frankly, where the cruise goes, it's just more fun for lesbians to be on a trip that caters to lesbians, in a world where lesbians, for once, are in the majority.

The entertainers laugh with, not at us, and the whole experience is wrapped up in a professional, well-run adventure. If you've never been, please consider it at least once. They have payment plans to help you make it work. Thank you for indulging my opinion, and now back to our regularly scheduled column.

I was really nervous about performing on the cruise, for people from all over the country (the world, actually), wondering if my Rehoboth experiences would resonate. Before the show some people wondered if *Aging Gracelessly* meant they were in for a discourse on geriatric medical issues or even a sex talk because of the *50 Shades* reference. Bonnie ran backstage laughing to tell me that one.

But in the end, the show worked, and I was so appreciative. My favorite part was hearing from young women all the following week how they enjoyed the stories from our old outlaw days and thanked all of us oldsters for our work for equality. Very satisfying.

I did suggest to my homies aboard that next time we need a map on our Rehoboth T-shirts, as nobody west of Pennsylvania (or east of the Atlantic Ocean) had a clue where Delaware was located.

Cruise behind us, we checked into our Pompano Beach lodging. I don't want to say Pompano is full of old people, but here, when the party's over and they chuck empty cans from the car, it's not Budweiser, it's Ensure.

Honest, Windsor and I saw the evidence on our morning walk.

And I do miss my progressive community. Yesterday at the pool, a woman asked the stereotypical, "Are you two sisters?"

"No," I said, "spouses."

She thought about it for a second or two. "Oh, in-laws!" she announced, certain she'd gotten it right. We gave up.

So do you remember Carole King's 2005 *Living Room Tour?* Now I'm doing one. On Saturday I've got a living room gig at a friend's Fort Lauderdale condo, and then a show on a Vero Beach pool deck. It's cool playing private parties, but of course we're schlepping the sound system, props, barstool, and giant Cosmo, like the senior citizen roadies we are.

By the way, rock 'n' roll lore defines roadies as the ones who set up and take down the technical stuff, while groupies are fans who sleep with the talent. From the look of our flaked-out family this morning, Bonnie and Windsor are roadies *and* groupies. By the time you read this, we will have packed up the circus, left the East Coast of Florida, and headed west for another month as snowbirds.

I admit I'm happy to miss the cold weather, snow closings, and television announcements noting "Peter and Paul, two hours late," or, my favorite, from the chicken plant, "Eviscerator crew, second shift canceled." Um, no eggs for me today, thanks.

So the *Aging Gracelessly* tour continues. We just got word that I'm booked into the historic Duplex Cabaret Theatre on Christopher Street this coming May. Now that's exciting!

In the meantime, if you're traveling and catch sight of the old Schnauzermobile, piled high with sound equipment and two aging roadies fixing to set up or tear down a gig, wave as you go by. The empty Ensure cans flung from the vehicle may just be ours.

March 2016

I love the irony of living in a trailer park (okay, manufactured home) with two luxury cars on the driveway. That each vehicle is over ten years old so we could afford them is fine with me.

But when one of our 2004 computerized car key fobs broke, I had to visit a fancy-shmancy car lot in Florida. When we pulled up in front of the local Lexus dealership I thought I was at the Dubai Hilton. The towering edifice covered more than a city block.

I looked for the Parts Department sign, envisioning the customary dark back room with a long Formica counter, staffed by a guy in a greasy Eagles hat. Nope. I found an adjacent freestanding airplane hangar with a cadre of tablet-using young professionals poised to greet us. One chipper young man ushered us into the war room, with 26 computer stations, (seriously, I counted!) each easily equipped to control air traffic into Chicago O'Hare. Over every desk in the place were framed diplomas from Lexus College. It made me wonder if my combined SAT score would have been enough to matriculate.

As we glided across the Italian marble tile, our caseworker assessed the damaged key. He logged us into the system on his iPad, then sent a lackey to fetch our car and spirit it away. Our counselor told us to enjoy our time in the lounge—estimated wait, two hours. For a *key*?????

We took the elevator to the second-floor lounge, where we discovered a half-dozen vibrating massage chairs in front of three massive flat-screen TVs. That they all were showing a bloviating Donald Trump had me shaking all over without a massage chair. There was also a beautiful boutique with logo clothing and expensive logo jewelry. Logo dog clothing, anyone? My favorite amenity was a lush putting green with complimentary clubs. I was tempted to grab one and smash at the Donald-occupied TV screens.

Oh, and there were aisles of greeting cards, which was good, as I suspected you could be there from one Easter to the next.

No decade-old *Time* magazines and vending machines here. There was a deco-designed snack bar with ten-stool seating, offering a variety of burgers and beverages. It looked like a set from *Happy Days*.

Meanwhile, as if we were waiting in the hospital surgical lounge, you could follow a massive video screen showing whether the "patient" was in surgery, recovery, or waiting to be discharged. In this case, the last step was a complimentary bath (and nail trim?)

Curious about the new car showroom, we descended to Level One, walked across campus and entered the gallery of dreams. Not only did we find ten awesome new vehicles on display under complex light shows, but we ran into a second elaborate snack and coffee bar, plus an adjacent lounge with several people waiting.

"See that old woman with the walker?" I asked. "Broke her key fob and she's been here since she was a teenager."

Also on the showroom floor was a battery-operated, perfectly scaled plastic replica luxury car for toddlers. It cost $499. Yup, five hundred bucks for a kids' toy. All I could do was cluck my tongue.

As for the new cars themselves, of course they were gorgeous, with amenities including dashboard computers I could use to write this column. Naturally, Bonnie checked out the engines and tires, while I ogled the lush interiors and multiple cup-holders.

I'm pretty sure the display models were equipped with wire-less eyeball recognition software since the instant I gazed at a car, a roving pack of salespersons flowed our way. Sadly, the cars cost roughly the value of our manufactured home. Some, many thousands more.

Finally, we were notified that our newly washed jalopy was coming off the line, ready for delivery, along with our brand-new key fob. The bill was $275. *For a key????*

Stunned, we leapt into the car and drove off. As we bid a fond farewell to Lexusland, Bonnie surprised me.

"I'd love to get you that shiny black Lexus for our anniversary."

"Awww," I responded.

"Yeah, but I don't have the $499."

Everybody's a comedian.

April 2016

Spring is closing in and I'm glad. Maybe if I spend some time outdoors I can escape my digital devices, which are sadly smarter than I am. It's been a long winter juggling smartphones, smart TVs, smart calorie counters, and smart remarks from my spouse to "put that thing away at the dinner table."

I never thought I'd become a digital junkie—somebody tethered to electronics, texting not calling, surfing, streaming, and relying on GPS to get to places I used to know how to find all by myself.

Frankly, I think my senior moments are caused by over-reliance on these glorious gizmos. In fact, they should be called digital dumb-downs because the more they do for us the less we can do for ourselves. If I get one more device to simplify my adult life, I'll be back in the playpen with a Fischer Price Plug 'N Play.

Take my smartphone. Please. I do love it, but its tragic flaw hit home last week when its battery died mid-call. My antique land-line was useless since I had no earthly idea how to call my best friend back. Her number was entombed in the deceased phone. The irony is, I can still spout by rote my junior high phone number: DAvis 2-1628. Yes, we had letters to start, no area codes, and good memories. Now, my smartphone has made my memory superfluous. The phrase "use it or lose it" comes to what's left of my mind.

My TV is also too smart for its own good. I got a device that can stream content from my phone to the 48-inch Sony. While I've been streaming movies for a couple of years now, this new gadget lets me stream from the whole Internet, including YouTube. Watching a 21-year-old Babs Streisand on the *Ed Sullivan Show*, Billy Joel when he still had a head of hair, and 1980s *Cagney and Lacey* episodes had me planted in front of the boob tube for days on end like a drooling zombie. If the TV was truly smart, it would have told me to turn it off and go to bed already.

But my latest obsession in smart technology is the digital step counter. When my low-tech pedometer fell off my shoe, I stepped on it, doing crunches (but not the kind that firm my abs). Then, my fancy rubber wristband step-counter turned my hand bile green. So I downloaded a step-counting app to my smart phone. That worked great, but the phone has to be in my pocket to work, so it missed some of my exertion.

Well, ladies and gentlemen, I found a solution. The 2016 Electronics Show in Las Vegas recently introduced the world's first (wait for it) . . . smart bra. Yes, people, the grand-mammary of all smart devices is a brassiere. According to the manufacturer, it measures your biometrics, like heart rate, oxygen level and steps, through a piece of clothing already worn daily.

I'll say. While I've been prone to leave my phone or pedometer home, this is one item where nobody has to warn me, "Don't leave home without it."

But how does this new kind of boob tube work? I'm always pulling out my phone to see how far I've trekked. If I check my smart bra at the mall will I be cited for indecent exposure? How reliable is this "bra counter"? Will it, dare I say, hold up?

The whole concept just leaves me hanging. How can an underwire bra also be wireless? And along with the regular support it provides, will it have tech support? And it better have long battery life, as I shudder to think about plugging my undergarment in at the airport.

Hey, maybe they can engineer the bra to speak, reporting blood pressure and heart rate like a GPS. Imagine hearing that emotionless dashboard voice broadcasting your vital signs to the world as it lifts and separates. Your data will no longer be just Victoria's secret.

So in light of our constantly evolving digital universe, I'm going to step back just a little for my sanity. In case of emergency, I've handwritten my important phone numbers into an old-fashioned paper address book. And while I am free to stream episodes of *The Sonny and Cher Show* or *Here Come the Monkees* on my TV, I'm going to try and stifle myself.

But when it comes to my fitness regimen, I'm going to give the smart bra a try. It's set to be released for sale shortly. I guess I'll have a choice of cup size, battery size, strapless, wireless, push-up or plug-in.

So I'm off to charge my bra. With my Visa card. When it arrives I can charge it again in the electric socket. It's all so 2016.

May 2016

HOW THE MOTHER OF ALL HOLIDAYS GOT ITS START

In honor of the approaching Mother's Day holiday, I'm celebrating mothers everywhere—mothers I've happily become, mothers I'm horrified I've become, and my own 86-year-old step-mom, who I'd like to become.

Sitting here at this motherboard (wow, that was a stretch), I can be heard snarking at the dog, "Don't make that face at me; a big wind will come along and freeze it that way."

At least I don't have to tell him to sit up straight.

Ah, Mother's Day. According to Internet historians, the holiday tradition started here in the motherland in the 1850s. One of our foremothers, West Virginia women's organizer Anna Reeves Jarvis, held Mother's Day work clubs to improve sanitary conditions, trying to lower infant mortality. Then, the motherly groups tended wounded soldiers from both sides during the Civil War and later held Mother's Friendship Day picnics to unite former enemies.

By 1908 Anna Jarvis' daughter, also named Anna Jarvis, thought her mother deserved a special day, so she created Mother's Day; see where the apostrophe is in "mother's"? It was just for her mother. And it was so talked about in her hometown that the tradition spread like a rash, becoming a national holiday by 1914.

Apparently over the years Anna thought better of it when she couldn't get a dinner reservation anywhere on her special day. And, she watched, horrified, as the price of the mother of all Mother's Day gifts, the Whitman Sampler (1915), skyrocketed. That's when she started to decry the commercialization of Mother's Day and spent the rest of her life trying to get the mother#&%$* holiday annulled. Seriously.

Others, however, embraced it as the mother lode—Hallmark (founded 1910), FTD-Florists Telegraph Delivery (1910 as well . . . coincidence???) and, of course, restaurants for Mother's Day brunches. Manhattan's Plaza Hotel (est. 1907), and, along the transcontinental railroad line, the Harvey House chain (America's first?) were jam-packed for Mother's Day from the beginning. San Francisco's dining room at the Majestic Hotel survived the 1906 earthquake only to suffer a four-hour wait on Mother's Day ever after.

For fried clam lovers, by 1925, you couldn't get a Mother's Day reservation at that new Howard Johnson's, either.

Anyone from the Maryland/D.C. area in the '60s and '70s will recall Mother's Day at Peter Pan Restaurant in Urbana, Md. You waited an eternity among wailing children and live pea fowl with fanning feathers, until they summoned you via screechy loudspeaker. I still remember the revolving relish tray with yummy apple butter and the enormous fried chicken breasts—the mothership of Mother's Day eats.

Today, Anna Jarvis would be seriously pissed, because unless you make your reservations for one of the Delaware coast's plethora of exceptional restaurants right now, you won't get a reservation this year, either. But I digress.

I'm a mother all right. I tell the dog, "don't put that in your mouth, you don't know where it's been," as well as the slightly edited anthem, "If you don't stop barking I'll give you something to bark about."

Yup, that's me, with classic mother mouth.

At the dog groomer: "A little soap and water never killed anybody."

At the dog superstore: "Do you think I'm made of money?"

At the dog park: "I don't care who started it, *you* stop it!"

About new kibble: "How do you know you don't like it if you haven't tasted it?"

And my favorite: "So it's raining? You're not sugar—you won't melt."

If my dog had opposable thumbs I could holler, "Pick it up yourself; are your paws broken?" or the quintessential "Close the door! I'm not air-conditioning the whole neighborhood!"

Mercifully, the only way I'd get to say, "Are you going out dressed like that?" is if I, myself, put him in a studded dog-collar and "Who Let the Dogs Out" T-shirt.

But let me explain why I want to be like my step-mom. At age 75 she got a computer. Which, of course, meant I got daily tech support calls. Then, at age 85, she got an iPhone. On one of her early calls to me she inadvertently pressed Face Time and I answered the call from the bathroom throne. Embarrassing!

And she texts. While 21st century language like OMG and LOL are not in her lexicon, she does let me know when she gets home from the museum, the theatre, or her Pilates class. Seriously, Pilates.

But my favorite momism happened at our winter rental house in Florida. One night, my spouse and I headed out to our darkened, private pool, threw abandon, not to mention *Vanity Fair*, to the wind and plunged into the (heated) water in our birthday suits.

Five minutes later, here comes mom, wearing only a beach towel, which she leaves behind to join us in the pool.

"Wheee!" she giggles, "I haven't done this in 70 years!"

I want to be just like her when I grow up.

In the meantime, enjoy Mother's Day, whether you spend it waiting for your electronic device to buzz, alerting you that your table is ready—or if you honor your mom or your kids honor you in other fun ways.

However you spend it, have a blast and give a nod to Anna Reeves Jarvis. I'll let you know where the dog scored a reservation to take us for dinner.

May 2016

RUDE NATION

Like the characters Velma and Roxie from the musical Chicago sing, "Whatever happened to class?"

It's a lost art.

I mention this mostly because of Donald Trump. He has ignited a giant, oozing mass of boorish, classless, disrespectful voters, bent on dividing, stigmatizing and making it all right, if not downright popular, to express hatred. And I've had some sad examples presented to me recently.

I was outside a restaurant, having a hard time finding a parking place, when I saw a car with its backup lights on, sitting, idling in place. I sat there behind the vehicle, watching for a full minute and then politely asked the driver, "Are you leaving?"

The driver spat, "I'm looking something up on the GPS. This space belongs to me until I decide to leave it!"

Wow. That's a lot of energy spent on random hostility. Oh, and his car wore a Trump bumper sticker.

Then one day I walked into an empty restaurant with hours posted as 11:30 a.m. to 9 p.m. It was a quarter to noon. A grumpy guy hollered from the back, admonishing me for being there by saying, "I just opened, still have to set up, and I have twenty minutes of work to do. I can't wait on anybody yet."

I squelched the urge to suggest he re-post his hours as 12:05-9.

And if those two incidents didn't push my buttons enough, I walked into an elevator down in Fort Lauderdale and said, with a smile, to the woman leaning her belly against the panel with the floor numbers on it, "Could you please press three for me?"

"I'm not the elevator operator!" she shot back, showing no willingness to move so I could push my own buttons.

I backed out and took the steps.

Of course, when discussing hateful and boorish, how can we ignore the recent North Carolina bathroom law? In the world of fantasy problems invented just to marginalize transgender people wanting to pee, this one is classic. Innocent children have a greater chance of being molested by a Republican lawmaker than by a transgender individual. And that's based on actual facts. Where do you pee, Dennis Hastert? Okay, I'm pissed, but at least I can be so and do so in the bathroom of my choice.

But just when I was ready to declare boorishness the new black, I thought about Hank and Ronnie, nonagenarian guests I met at a motel in Florida. They were both about five feet short and spry. On the day we talked, they were being interviewed by a local magazine to celebrate their seventy-second wedding anniversary.

"It's really only thirty-six years," Ronnie offered, "because I only listen to him half the time."

At that point Hank comes over to our spot by the pool, a violin on his shoulder, and plays "Blue Skies." Ronnie stops doing handstands in the pool to warn us to "be safe and stay out of the way of the dropped notes."

"Watch it," says Hank to Ronnie, "the anniversary is next week. We may not make it."

Then, completely un-coached, they asked us "How long have you two been together?" applauding when we said, "34 years this month."

Then Ronnie invited us back to their room the following evening for a violin concert, a little George and Gracie Allen routine, and potent vodka drinks to toast to our anniversaries.

In their case, civility and class were not dead and even vaudeville was alive and kicking.

Then, only a few weeks later, we had more of our faith renewed. We reached the front door of a popular New Orleans restaurant and were told by the host, "I've just seated six people and I'm putting you two at the end of the eight-top with them."

Uh-oh. Could be awkward.

We arrive at the table to greet six good-looking twenty-somethings in three heterosexual pairings.

Uh-oh. Could be really awkward.

We make introductions, warm up to conversations about

occupations and vacations, and order our classic fried chicken and red beans and rice. Pretty soon it's clear that beer mugs are being hoisted in honor of the impending marriage of one of the couples and recent engagement of another.

I flung caution to the wind and announced to the celebrants, "I hope you will be as happy as we have been for the past 34 years—and you'll look back fondly at this dinner with the two old lesbians at the end of the table."

Laughter ensued, followed by selfies and requests for the waiter to get all of us in a photo. It was fun and greatly encouraging on the class and anti-boorishness front.

Then again, I just saw "The Donald" on TV telling us how smart he is, denigrating immigrants, and revving up his disciples to go forth and hate anybody who isn't exactly like them.

It won't be easy to get those worms back into the can.

May 2016
PARDON ME, I HAVE TO GO VACUUM THE GRASS

Things have changed. When lots of us got to the beach between ten and twenty years ago, our wave of D.C./Philly/Baltimore/ Jersey transplants were in our mid-forties to early fifties. And there were a lot of us, all about the same age group. Okay, I guess the baby boom had descended on Rehoboth Beach.

Of course, there were adventurous people our age here before us, and a generation of gay people here before them, too—and many more pioneers before that. But in earlier years our community was less out, less visible. And sadly, in that earlier decade, mid-1980s to mid-1990s, the AIDS epidemic seriously struck the Rehoboth community of guys, while many of the gals were here or still in the big cities doing what they could to help their brothers.

But by 1993-95 the baby *kaboom* arrived, weekending and commuting at first, but then, mostly two by two, moving to the beach permanently. The guys and some gals gathered at the now-defunct big dance club, The Renegade, the girls had our beloved Friday night happy hours at the also-gone Cloud 9 Bar, we all ate the best chicken salad on earth from Lori's Deli (still here!) and hung out at the CAMP Courtyard—even when it was only half the size it is now. But it did have that gorgeous rainbow picket fence.

And, let's face it. We were youngish, eager for do-it-ourselves yard work or home improvement projects, rabid to volunteer for events until 11 p.m., then go for a nightcap or breakfast at midnight. Of course, we could dance to Donna Summer or Cher for days. And still get up the next day bright and early for work or play. Those were the days, my friends.

Now I am not claiming complete decrepitude. But today, as Bonnie and I drove home from Lowes with five 60-pound bags of sand and thirty concrete patio tiles, we agreed that things were different. It now takes us the same time to fix up our postage stamp yard at the House of Windsor as it used to take us to landscape, mulch and mow the three-quarter acre manse at Schnauzerhaven.

When we got home, we had to team up to hoist the 60-pound sand bags from the car and in unison do an ungainly crabwalk to transfer the bags to the backyard. It reminded me of a three-legged race at a company picnic.

As for the concrete pavers, carrying one was manageable, but two were potential emergency-room visits. So I made thirty trips between driveway and yard, leaning the concrete on my handy protruding belly as I traveled.

The job took forty-five minutes and registered 1.3 miles on the pedometer. It's not my best time, but I had to stop for huffing, puffing, and kvetching. So yeah, as retirees we've got plenty of time, but then everything takes plenty of time.

My favorite part of the yard cleanup was tending to the grass. While Bonnie mowed the tiny patch of real grass with our small electric mower (anybody want to do a lottery on what date this summer we run over the cord?), I took the Shop-Vac to the rest of the "lawn."

Yes, in an effort to encourage Windsor to try something new, we installed artificial turf in two tiny areas. It works great. Liquid drains to the stones and earth below and solids get poop patrolled like the rest of the yard. It cuts down on mowing, but it is weird going out to vacuum the grass.

Is it me, or are bags of mulch heavier than they used to be? And do these heavier bags seem to contain less Premium Black Shredded Hardwood? So far, in two trips, we've schlepped 22 deadweight bags from Lowes to the house and it's not enough. People, I don't live at Downton Abbey.

Although, in the morning, I suspect I'll feel as if I mulched the north forty. Next time I'm just going to spread shredded dollar bills in the flowerbeds. It should work just as well, save a trip to the chiropractor, and consequently cost less.

But don't get me wrong. Bonnie and I still love our little manufactured home (with its tiny backyard of manufactured lawn) and life is good, good, good.

And here's the most encouraging news. The younger generation is here! We've seen ample evidence at the bars, dog-walking, out to dinner, and all over town. Awesome forty- and fifty-hsomethings, representing all the letters in LGBT, are doing the weekending/commuting, dancing, volunteering, home improvement projects, and keeping those late-night venues in business.

We love you! But that certainly doesn't mean we're anywhere near ready to cede our barstools, volunteer badges, or tix to events big and small. We're still here, still queer, and pretty damn used to it. And the more things change, the more they stay the same. I love it.

June 2016
BEAUTY SECRETS FROM "THE FINGERNAIL FILES"

As I sit writing this, it's United Nations World Happiness Day. Clearly those who suggested the holiday have not been watching the U.S. presidential primary coverage. Although it does square with the news that the U.S. ranks 13th in world happiness, whereas Denmark is first. Obviously, Shakespeare aside, nothing is rotten in Denmark.

As for me, this past week I decided to de-stress myself from current events and advance the U.S. happiness scale by taking some much needed "me" time.

Following a hair appointment to color and highlight my prematurely gray hair (are my pants on fire?), I figured a massage would further relax me.

"Hello, before I usher you into our waiting lounge, do you need to use the restroom?"

"Nope."

So then the sadist receptionist brings me into a darkened room with a loudly tinkling water feature. "Um, about that bathroom . . ."

Returning, I saw a table with jars of aromatherapy sprigs. I sniffed one titled "Contentment" and it smelled like Pennzoil. Going in for a sniff of "Relaxation," I leapt back, face and nose contorted by the olfactory assault. Jeesh, if that was relaxation how does "Hassle" smell?

Then a staffer asked me to turn off my cell phone.

"And you want me to relax????"

I lay on the table in the dimly lit room, listening to melody-free music, trying to unclench my body. It was tough not to recall medical exams. Or the first massage I'd ever had—where an 80-year-old Nordic masseuse poured so much oil on me I expected her to add tomatoes and balsamic vinegar.

"Hello," said the seemingly teenage masseuse. As she worked on me, I tried to engage her in conversation, but was met with one-word answers. "Jersey," "Cool," "Adele." The single multi-syllable response was to my question, "How long have you been doing this?" with the answer being "Fifteen minutes." Last comic kneading.

Admittedly very relaxed, I rose cautiously from the table, dressed slowly and exited in a leisurely manner. I was afraid to step out into reality and traffic too fast lest I get the bends. Luckily there was a nail salon next door so I could continue the pamperfest.

My nail polish history is an American horror story. While an infrequent activity, I would occasionally head to the salon. Despite foraging for credit card and keys pre-manicure so as not to use my hands afterwards, without fail, within minutes I looked like somebody who'd clawed their way out of a building collapse. Ten bucks down the crapper.

But this time, I learned something astonishing. The technician told me about gel polish, guaranteed to dry instantly, be strong as an ox and endure several weeks without chipping. And the cost was only twenty dollars more than regular polish. Perfect!

I chose an uncharacteristic Reese Witherspoon pink for my nails and let the techie have at it. It was a simple procedure, pre-paid so as not to disturb the polish when I left.

So far, so good. But as I stepped out into the parking lot, my phone rang. Physiologically unable to ignore a ringing phone, I rooted around in my pocket for the device, took the call and amazingly did not screw up a single fingernail. This was incredible. They stayed perfect. Magic gel! I was sold. My world happiness score jumped several notches.

It was not until I showed off my nails to a woman entering the salon that I learned the truth. Hearing it was my first gel polish experience, she asked if the technician mentioned that you can't remove the gel polish by yourself. *Excuse me?* You have to come back? That's right, after the fact, I learned that cotton balls and polish remover are useless, as my digits were now encased in rock-solid gel to be removed only by a professional—the ultimate case of "don't try this at home."

That's when I started to suspect that this fingernail gel coat was the exact same substance used to paint fiberglass boat hulls. I could have smashed a bottle of champagne on my thumb and it would still be in the pink. I'd have to go to a marine detailer to get this gunk off.

When I got home and googled gel nail polish, I became alarmed. Blog after blog reported the sordid dangers of gel nails. How "a long chain of molecules in the gel polishes gives them strength, hardened by exposure to ultraviolet light."

Ah yes, now I recall having my hands placed under a glowing purple haze. Was the UV curing step a road to "cumulative DNA damage, premature skin aging and even cancer?" Oh boy.

Article after article advised applying SPF 50 sunscreen before a manicure or wearing protective gloves with the fingertips cut off. Somehow I cannot see me wearing weight-lifting gloves into the salon. But I certainly didn't want premature age spots to go with my prematurely gray hair.

Other articles cautioned leaving nails unpolished (*Oh no! Not that!*) for at least two weeks between gel coats to assess nail condition and prevent infections. Then there's the danger of peeling and lifting, where water can seep into the nail, leading to thinning of the nail plate and a dreaded fungus. Not one to encourage a fungus among us (sorry), this all seemed very complicated to me.

With all the other things I've got to worry about, I couldn't see myself obsessing over abscesses in my nail beds. These babies looked great.

My shiny nails glowed pretty in pink as I sat before the TV to catch up on the news. Oy, there was violence on the campaign trail! Lead in the water! Deadly Zika virus! Children with guns!

No wonder America is unlucky number thirteen in world happiness. Clenched up, stressed to the max, I sat watching the babbling talking heads on TV, my nails digging into my thighs.

My relaxation was long gone, but at least my gel coat was here to stay.

June 2016

PASSING THE PRIDE ALONG

It's Pride season, although I am proud to live in a place where we celebrate all year long. But recently there's been a lot of talk about our gay culture and whether we might lose it by gaining our rights and disappearing into the swiftly moving mainstream.

Judy Garland, Walt Whitman, Billie Jean King, *Rubyfruit Jungle*, drag kings, Harvey Milk, P-town. Our history, our heroes, our catch phrases, our culture. We have a long past featuring a common sensibility born from our outlaw days as a secret society.

We managed to survive and even thrive while much of society despised us. We have our jokes, etiquette, magazines, and buzzwords. But I worry. How does this culture survive and get handed down?

In most cultures, passing along the history and sensibility is the job of the parents, grandparents, aunts, and uncles. My Jewish family taught me my culture. From as far back as I can remember there was chopped liver, matzo ball soup, and hand-wringing guilt; Grandma Rose taught me to make blintzes, Uncle Abe couldn't stop telling Henny Youngman jokes, and of course we learned our social history ("Never again!")

By the time I was ten, I was thoroughly steeped in our Jewish ethos. It was our culture to learn and to savor, handed down at the dinner table.

Which begs the question How the heck are we going to make sure our gay culture gets passed down through generations if our alphabet generations do not, for the most part, come from LGBT parents?

Wake up, people, it's our job! Yes, each of us. We've each got to be a storehouse, a library, and an oral history of LGBT knowledge, trivia, and even jokes.

How many lesbians does it take to change a lightbulb?

Six. One to change the bulb and five more to sit around and process. (*Rim shot sound effect.*)

We need to go back and embrace our early years. Let's hear it for The Mattachine Society, Harry Hay, and Leonard Matlovich. Don't know about them? Find out! Let's talk about lesbian separatists, like the Gutter Dykes in Berkeley, and Radicalesbians in Manhattan. And tales of U.S. properties owned by women where only women were allowed. They would even take *m-e-n*, out of it completely, spelling it *wimmin* or *womyn*.

My favorites were The Van Dykes, a roving band of van-driving vegans who shaved their heads, refused to speak to men, and traveled the highways stopping only on "Women's Land."

In the '80s we had the Pink Panthers protecting neighborhoods from anti-gay violence, gay credit unions, stores, publishing houses, and late great gay bookstores. The first organized lesbian group, the Daughters of Bilitis, had a name that sounded like a disease, but it was powerful. Pass it on!

We must broadcast the work of the Gay Men's Health Crisis, the enormity of the AIDS quilt, the pioneers like Barbara Gittings and Frank Kameny who picketed the White House in the '60s for gay rights, the fall of "Don't Ask, Don't Tell," and the entire equality playbook that has brought us to this Pride season. This is culture we need to protect, celebrate, and hand down to our youngsters.

Do we institute "Take a Baby Dyke to Lunch Week"? Well, maybe. Not only can we pass along what we know to those younger than we are, but we can socialize with our elders and solicit their stories before they are lost to time.

I have been lucky, as a writer, to interview so many people over the years and hear about their remarkable lives. I was astounded in speaking with one late gay elder, a retired bartender at a long-gone gay bar. I was shocked and saddened when I heard his tale of being arrested, jailed, and permanently stripped of his teaching license because he was caught in a gay relationship.

These things mostly didn't happen anymore in my generation (fired, yes; jail, not so much), but they happened frequently and tragically to our previous generations. We need to know the stories and pass them along.

With not as many everyday softball leagues as there used to be, we're in danger of forgetting that softball was one of the premier ways lesbians used to meet. Leagues were ubiquitous and as important to our tribe as gay bars. Not so much today.

Whether we have been in touch with our families of origin or not, most of us have built marvelous families of affinity with whom we share holidays, birthdays and daily living. Let's widen the circle to include Gen X, Millennials, Gen Z, and whatever generations we do not represent. We can spread the word and preserve our culture.

And we shouldn't leave out the fun stuff, either.

How many lesbians does it take to change a light bulb?

Six. One to change the bulb and five more to organize the potluck.

We need to make sure tales of the 1979 march, TV's Ellen coming out, films like *Desert Hearts,* and our fabled Women's Music live on. Our gay pioneers meant it's possible for Ricky Martin, the Indigo Girls, and Sam Smith to be out and proud now. So go join a P-Flag chapter. Get involved. Encourage multi-generational get-togethers to share and perpetuate our culture. Be the voice to share our antiquity.

After all, who, if not us, will keep the memory of the mullet haircut alive. It's part of our culture. Embrace it. And be glad it's gone.

June 2016

Pride month has always been a time to celebrate. And after the events of June 12 in Orlando, when a gay safe haven was violated, we must mourn, support our community, and then move on. Or else the haters win. And we cannot let them win. Not the anti-gay haters or the anti-American haters. We cannot let them win.

Yes, I'm sad and angry. No, I am not callous and wishing we could just move on. Yes, I could easily stay depressed over the loss of those precious lives and be scared for myself, my community, my gay life. But I won't.

There are plenty of voices raised in sorrow, anger and not a little fear for our safety. Plenty raised in solidarity, prayer, and mourning. Not me. I'll use this ink, this magazine page I am generously given to ask you to join me in trying to effect change.

What needs to be changed? First, LGBT visibility. And it translates to safety. Come out, come out, whoever you are. Everybody needs to come out, again and again. The more people see us and know us, the safer we will be. Legislation alone, while critically important, cannot protect LGBT people.

A straight friend once said, "You have your rights now, it's great, right? What else do you need?"

We need respect. Clearly we are still not safe from hatred fomented from some pulpits and wedge issue- seeking politicians. Clearly respect and a safe environment cannot be legislated. So all of us, gay and our allies alike, must bravely come out to everyone we encounter in support of respect for LGBT Americans.

We must speak up, outing ourselves, introducing spouses, and nonchalantly educating society. It will make us safer.

Second, we must make guns safer. Ha! You laugh! It's a non-starter! At the moment, it is. As President Obama just said, we've made cars safer, saving countless lives with safety improvements. And nobody is yelling "They're going to take away our cars!"

We're allowed to have conversations about auto safety. So we have, and cars are safer.

Now we must fight the NRA and the right-wing political machine for conversations about gun safety. We must demand these conversations. If we could talk about it, we'd encourage fingerprint ID technology on guns. It would prevent gun owners from having their own weapons yanked out of their hands and used to kill them; toddlers finding a gun and killing a sibling; criminals stealing guns and using them to kill. The tech is on our iPhones; why not our guns?

If we could talk about it, we'd discuss background checks so suspected terrorists on the no-fly list couldn't buy guns. The hypocrisy is stunning. You cannot claim to hate potential terrorists while telling them to buy all the guns they want. Demand to talk about this!

Shout it out: Assault weapons are only for killing humans—and a lot of them at a time. What place does this have off the battlefield? Ban them again. We must have this conversation.

By the way, the government is not coming for your guns. That battle cry is a despicable right-wing red herring. Cowboys, businesspeople, farmers, hunters and even a raging liberal like me who likes sport shooting, should be allowed to keep our guns. But demand a conversation about safety!

Third, make sure we do not let the dividers and haters encourage us to do their work for them. We cannot scapegoat the entire Muslim-American community, or even immigrating refugees, for the heinous deeds of some hate-filled, disturbed individuals.

The more we broad-brush the Muslim community with the taint of the few, and the more we marginalize members of an entire religion, the more incentive there is for young, disaffected persons to seek misguided fame.

We must not hate. There must be room for all. It's safer that way.

How do we do it? The coming out portion is direct, although not always easy. Like Nike says, just do it. Be fearless, be friendly, but be out. When people get to know us personally, we are no longer just "one of them." Do it. Eventually it will even be fun.

The gun safety conversations? DEMAND them . . . sign a petition, demand it of your legislators, write a letter to the editor, talk on social media, join the Brady Campaign to Prevent Gun Violence (bradycampaign.com), speak out!

And finally, make "Room for All" your credo. Hopefully, we can reach out to our Muslim neighbors, work to be inclusive, learn about their community, and respect them as we too wish to be respected. Will we achieve total success? Of course not. Will this stop all discrimination against the LGBT and Muslim communities? No way. Will this curb all gun violence? I'm not that naïve.

But if we all work together, we can have the conversations that lead to real change. If we do our part, we can go back to celebrating Gay Pride Month the way it was meant to be celebrated. Because if the gay community has learned one thing over the years, it's that *silence = death.*

June 2016

I just read a report that one of the major airlines has decided that culinary deprivation is not friendly customer service. They will be providing passengers with snacks again. Like that would help.

For a person raised in the era when you could get to the airport forty-five minutes before your flight, check two heavy bags for free, and carry on as many ounces of liquid refreshment and/or moisturizing cream as you wanted, peanuts are not going to cut it.

We used to fly standby, be allowed to pack scissors, have family walk us to the gate, enjoy an onboard meal, fly in relative comfort, and have loved ones greet us the moment we landed. Those were the good old days.

Okay, I do not miss the sexism of the whole stewardess thing, and I love that flight attendants come in all manner of age, gender, race, and sexual orientations. As wonderful as that evolution is, it doesn't make up for the tragic deterioration of modern air travel.

Not only can I now spend consecutive days in the same TSA line, enjoying a quarter of my trip at an airport, but I have to wear flip-flops to do it. That's because sneakers are too complex to put back on while hopping on one foot and grabbing my stuff off the moving conveyor belt. And God forbid I leave my bag unattended for a minute. I live in fear of airport personnel detonating my pajamas.

Frankly, I didn't miss snacks and wouldn't even miss beverages. Every time I balance a cocktail on my flimsy tray table the guy in front of me leans his seat back and shoots two ounces of booze up my nose—not the kind of vodka stinger I prefer.

I should decline drinks anyway, since it's hell to battle my way out of the middle seat, squeeze up the incredible shrinking aisle, and pray the restroom is available. My bladder isn't what it used to be. Remember when we'd laugh at the closed door and hope somebody was joining the mile high club? Now I'm terrified to laugh at all.

And even if I could snag an aisle seat, we're all now members of the mile-thigh club, haunches hanging over the teeny seats, obstructing the forward progress of the drink carts. I hate deplaning bruised and battered, having been sideswiped by a six-pack of Snapple.

So they think snacks will help? The headline on CNBC said, "Airlines get back to basics again."

Seriously? To me, basics are not Dutch-style, waffle-shaped cookies called "Stroopwafel," as the online article noted. To me, basics are legroom and my seat-mate's elbow out of my kidney.

One deluded airline employee noted, "We know that even the smallest detail can make a big difference in the travel experience." Really? How about a small detail like being able to exhale without arranging for the adjacent traveler to inhale?

Oh, and get this. The airlines are starting to free up these sugary Stroopwafels because . . . wait for it . . . the price of oil is cheaper! Seriously? Airlines think that doling out 40 million Stroopwafels (yes, I love writing that word) is a better choice than giving us another inch of knee room? Or another nonstop flight?

Ever since the adoption of the ubiquitous hub system, passengers have to fly through Atlanta to go anywhere at all. If you're going to hell you have to go through Atlanta first.

Although one thing I appreciate about flying these days is that flight attendants have developed a sense of humor. I overheard one recently announce, "In case of loss of cabin pressure, oxygen masks will descend. Stop screaming and put one over your face. If you have a small child with you, secure your mask before assisting with theirs. If you are traveling with more than one child, pick your favorite."

Another stand-up flight attendant warned, "There may be 50 ways to leave your lover but there are only two ways out of this plane. If it's a water landing, feel free to take your seat cushion as a souvenir."

Vaudeville aside, flying is not fun anymore. Between arm-wrestling for armrests and the game of "will I or won't I" get my bag into the overheads, it's torturous. I'm a white-knuckle flyer at best anyway, and fearing Ebola from the hacking cougher man-spreading into my personal space just adds to my angst. Returning my seat to an upright position should not risk breaking my nose.

So what are airlines doing to solve these pressing problems? Launching a snack attack, apparently. At this point the three biggest U.S. airlines have announced that free snacks are back, even in steerage.

Restoring complimentary snacks has been deemed the solution to all manner of airline customer complaints. The airlines call this "investing in the passenger experience." I call it investing in bakery products.

As for the customer experience, it's the Stroopwafel, the whole Stroopwafel, and nothing but the Stroopwafel.

June 2016

American Ninja Warrior: Those who can, do; those who can't, watch. And I've been watching.

Have you seen this show? Technically it's a reality show, but the level of athleticism needed to compete is astounding, making it a very fascinating program.

The athletes do the most challenging things, on an almost impossible and wacky obstacle course. I'm insanely impressed and love to watch the men and women do, what seems to me, the impossible. Well frankly, to me it is impossible.

Although, for most of the challenges, I can compete with them for my own personal bests.

One of the first Ninja challenges on the course is the ring jump over the pegs. Athletes dangle from a bar on two giant red rings, and use their entire body strength to leap up and over eight-inch-high pegs atop the pole. They travel that way, leaping and moving along toward the next challenge. Failure means dropping into water below.

For me this is not unlike my leaping up to hang stuff on my closet's severely too-high clothes rod. It takes my entire body strength to leap up and catch the plastic hanger on the bar. If the plastic hanger breaks, I go, not into the water, but into a pile of shoes. Water would hurt less.

It's a thrill to watch these muscular Ninja women hold onto a horizontal one-inch ledge with their heels, thighs and fingertips, then drop to a vertical position, holding on only by their fingertips. The announcers go crazy about the strength of their fingertips.

Have you ever tried to open a Tupperware container of dog kibble? Once that Tupperware has been burped, to reopen it takes the same Herculean fingertip strength those Ninjas use. Struggle for a while to pop the top without success and you'll wish for a dunking instead of the pitying look on the schnauzer face below.

They should have a Ninja challenge like the trial posed by my fancy new washing machine. The warrior would bend completely in half to retrieve a small object from a revolving drum, well below the tiny platform where they are perched.

I stand on a wobbly footstool, bent in half at the waist, flailing wildly, trying not to plummet headfirst into the washing machine, just to retrieve a wet pair of underpants. These new appliances are so bottomless that short people like me wind up on ladders, leaning down to retrieve socks with salad tongs.

I love to watch the Ninjas leap into midair to grab onto a swinging cylindrical boxing bag, landing on the tiniest ledge around it. It rivals my getting up a good head of steam, jumping onto the back of my giant rolling trash can, leaning back to the proper angle and propelling a week's worth of stinky garbage to the curb. *Wheeee! Go, Waste Management Warrior!*

Then there's the Warrior Escalator challenge. The contestant has to jump from step to moving step, legs almost horizontal, hoping not to miss a foothold and get dunked in the water.

It's really pretty similar to the happy dance I do in the yard to avoid puppy land mines. I repeat, landing in water would be better.

And finally, the Ninja Challenge course ends with the Great Wall. These mega-athletes take a running start and exercise a superhuman leap to propel themselves straight up a nearly vertical barrier. For the very few that make it, it's on to the finals.

Ha! They have nothing on me, leaping up the sheer face of the refrigerator hoping to open the cabinet above where I've hidden the Thin Mint Girl Scout cookies. For the very few times I make it, I'm on to the final wearing of my current size shorts.

Now in order to be cast on the program and to compete as a Ninja, there's a whole application process. First, you have to fill out an essay about why you want to compete. Frankly, I'm pretty sure I can handle that challenge. Second, they say that since it's a reality show, in addition to your physical training you must have a captivating backstory. What do you think? Mine sure wouldn't be the same old workout and physical fitness tale.

And finally, you have to send them a video of your training program and glimpse of your training regimen.

I'm in the process of doing a video selfie of me fishing for dish towels in the washing machine and executing my poop-dodging backyard choreography. I'll probably have to enlist the help of a videographer to film my two-handed Girl Scout cookie lunge and rescue.

All in all, American Ninja Warriors inspires my quest to stay fit and accomplish the activities of daily living. And it really entertains me. Maybe my video application can do the same for the show's producers.

Ready, set, hang up those pants! Film at eleven.

June 2016

ADVERTISING'S DISTURBING
CREATURE COMFORTERS

I'm here to talk about Big Pharma and the birth of the snot monster. Now I am so sorry to be this disgusting so early in my column, but I have just about had it with drug company commercials on TV. And the Snot Monster (his given name by the ad agency who birthed him) hawking the drug Mucinex is just the tip of the ice bag.

It's hard to believe that the agency which first came up with animated mucus did so a decade ago. Apparently, this terrible idea was born because nobody on TV was talking about mucus. Are we surprised?

So agency illustrators drew the little lumbering Mucus Man (not to be confused with the Broadway musical of a similar title) to waddle around, peddling the drug Mucinex.

And it worked. Really well. So, in the decade following that Green Blob's first gooey footsteps came a new era. Body parts and bodily functions morphed into endearing little anthropomorphic cartoon characters. Television has been overrun with bouncing body parts ever since.

From squirming, dancing bladders to creepy creatures representing sleep deprivation, these ads are the 21st century equivalent of highway accidents: You ought not stare but you cannot look away. I mean, how often do you get the chance to see a roiling lower intestine? Too often, I say.

The only good thing about this alarming advertising trend is that I am no longer able to eat while I watch TV, and that's a good thing. Prescription advertising mascots have curbed my appetite like no diet plan ever has. They've also curbed my enthusiasm for prime time, alas.

Face it, one minute you're watching football and the next there's a giant animated toenail on your 55-inch Sony, showing off its high-definition foot fungus. Say hello to the Jublia Big Toe.

If you ask me, this is advertising putting its very worst-looking foot forward. Quick, post a Fund Me page so this digit can get a pedicure to hide the fungus among us.

And what's with those critter-like fuzzy letters in the insomnia commercial? What the hell are they? Dogs? Cats? Mohair sweaters? Spelling out "W-A-K-E" and "S-L-E-E-P," we see little fuzzy Wake fight with little furry Sleep. I don't know whether to notify the Humane Society or the Grammar Police. Is it animal abuse or revenge of the nouns? Frankly, it's so creepy it keeps me up at night, which surely makes this drug contraindicated. Watch this weird commercial and you may never sleep again.

And we cannot ignore television's friendly little bladder-boy. That's right, a bouncy bladder buddy holds hands with a panic-stricken woman and drags her into a succession of public restrooms. I want to watch HGTV, not somebody's over-active bladder hijacking its human. Ewwww. I mean it's not the Syfy channel. Or is it?

As an aside to this bladder business, my pharmacological column research led me to an app for the iPhone called "RunPee." It's an app that summarizes movies and tells you when you can safely run to the bathroom without missing much. I'm serious. This is a real thing. RunPee. There is nothing I can say here that would be any more amusing than the name of this app and the fact that it exists.

But I digress.

Back on topic, we have the newest drug-pushing spokes-metaphor—the walking, squirming lower intestine. Yup, cutesy colon creature is brought to you by the drug Xifaxan. It's got a sweet turtle face and slinky body and pretty soon you are sitting there, thinking he's kind of cute and feeling sorry for him and . . . Wait a minute! You're feeling empathy with an irritable bowel? You should hate his guts. But there they are, the very guts, dancing, winking, playing on your emotions. It gives me Irritable Viewer Syndrome. Frankly, this guy might be both the literary and figurative bowels of this entire genre.

And why are we seeing these ads anyway? Most are for products you cannot even buy without going to the doctor for a prescription. Call me old-fashioned, but I would prefer the doctor recommend a drug for me, not the other way around. The drug manufacturers are banking on me going to the doctor to request a specific medication because I'm smitten with a talking intestine? It would be preposterous if it wasn't working.

And in fact, this whole business of pharmaceutical companies dealing drugs directly to patients, manipulating us with cutesy, often endearing creatures, makes me want to swallow a fistful of anxiety meds.

Of course, then I'd have to deal with the incessantly advertised side effects, which is another frightening thing about these kitschy commercials. Do I really want to take their sleeping pill if I have to worry about "narcolepsy, the danger of operating heavy machinery, confusion, hallucinations, memory loss, and next-day drowsiness"?

Hell, I can skip the medication altogether and earn all those side effects by operating the heaviest machinery I own—a blender—and downing an entire pitcher of margaritas.

Although adorable Mr. Liver may then have something to say about it.

July 2016

Author's note: the following speech was presented by me to the members of the Golden Crown Literary Society on Saturday morning, July 9, 2016. The GCLS is a nonprofit organization specifically for lesbian writers and their readers, celebrating the books we write and those who read them. My keynote address was on a topic dear to my heart, preserving gay culture, and as such, it may contain a line or three that you've read from me before. Also, it's a wee bit longer than the rest of the chapters in this book—so if you need a break for the necessary room, now would be a good time. But hurry back. I have stuff to say.

Good morning!

I'm so thrilled to be here with all of you to make this presentation at GCLS 2016. What a conference this is—so many incredible writers and readers coming together . . . and not on Facebook, actually face to face. It's novel. It's magical.

GCLS 2016. A decade ago, at GCLS 2006, I was first introduced to this organization and many of our wonderful members.

I came to Atlanta, not to represent myself, a first-time author, but to accept the posthumous Trailblazer Award for my dear friend and mentor Anyda Marchant, author of the 14 classic Sarah Aldridge novels.

She and her late partner of 57 years, Muriel Crawford, had been two of the four founders of the legendary Naiad Press and later, by themselves, A&M Books. They had both recently passed away, both in their 90s, and they left A&M Books to me.

I was a lesbian deer in the headlights. My only knowledge of publishing was what Anyda and Muriel taught me of their antiquated, non-computerized ways.

They kept their financials in stacks of hardcover account books, like Charles Dickens' Bob Cratchit. Their tools of the trade were yellow no. 2 pencils, legal pads, and tumblers of Dewar's Scotch. The only part I really understood was the liquor.

And the business was just a trickle of its former self. About five or six times a month, Anyda would slowly and carefully make her way to the freestanding garage adjacent to their house. She'd find the right carton among dozens and select the requested Sarah Aldridge book.

Then, back at the house, she and Muriel would wrap the book in brown paper and send it out to a reader who, by the way, had contacted them by snail mail, or sometimes the rotary phone, requesting one of the 14 still-in-print Sarah Aldridge novels. This wasn't 1976; it was 2006. Amazon? They had no clue.

When, just before she died, Anyda asked me to take over the business, I was honored and welcomed the job. But I was a totally accidental publisher.

My first collection of magazine columns had been published by Anyda and Muriel in 2004, and I figured the book would be a "one and done." And there was nothing else in the pipeline to be published by A&M Books. I expected to settle into the role of archivist and keeper of the flame, nothing more.

So when I came to GCLS that summer, I hadn't signed up to participate in panels or read my work, nothing. I was there simply for the tremendous honor being bestowed upon Anyda.

But a funny thing happened on A&M's way to publishing extinction. I was welcomed with open arms by a flock of really friendly and fascinating women, both readers and writers.

They were curious about my book, asked what I intended to publish next, and hoped they'd get to hear me read. A couple of the women hunted down a hotel alcove and, during a refreshment break, set me up to read. It wasn't until last week when I found an old photo from that day that I realized that two of the women in the picture are now my good friends, award-winning writers Lynn Ames and Ellen Hart.

They, and then Marianne K. Martin and Kelly Smith of Bywater Books at an early Saints & Sinners Literary Conference, took me under their wings, talked to me about lesbian publishing, and welcomed me to the community.

That I was nominally the competition bothered no one. In

fact, some of the heaviest hitters in this business, from Bella to Bold Strokes to Bywater Books, have gone out of their way to help me keep Anyda's publishing legacy alive and to help relaunch and reinvent A&M Books.

Of course, that meant a crash course for me in ISBN numbers, sell sheets, e-books, book spines, and beta readers. You've heard of drumming circles? We had bar code circles, sitting with friends, drinking cocktails, and stickering hundreds of books so we could sell them on Amazon.

Over the next eight years I published a new novel by early feminist icon Ann Allen Shockley, a terrific novel by television producer Stefani Deoul, a memoir by Lee Watton who had been kicked out of the military in the 1960s, and a new edition of the first Sarah Aldridge book *The Latecomer*, with essays by many legendary lesbian writers and entertainers—including some you see here today. I also published three more collections of my own columns.

It worked and was a blast, all nourished and helped by so many people in this room. And in fact, as of last summer, A&M Books became part of the Bywater Books family and I could not be more thrilled.

But now, in a really weird turn of events, in addition to my four published books, at age 68 I have a whole new career, as a professional storyteller.

Some of you may have seen my show last summer in New Orleans or to benefit GCLS in P-town. I've been touring with the show for over a year now.

This too is a direct result of GCLS and the lesbian publishing world. When I'd read my stories at the cons, audiences would laugh. Then they started to nag, asking me over and over when I was going to book myself as a stand-up comic.

Are you kidding? Break into show business? At my age I'd be just as likely to break a hip.

And I knew I was way too old to be up on my feet, bouncing around a stage with a microphone to my mouth for an hour. Besides, I can't remember my grocery list much less an hour of material.

So instead, I became a sit-down comic, reading my stories. It works. I've been called the "Last Comic Sitting." And I'm having a grand time. Who knows how long this show biz career will last, but it's fun.

And the future is what brings me to my actual point this morning. It's such an honor to be chosen to do this keynote, and a large responsibility, too. So I wondered what my actual message should be.

"You're going to be funny, right?" came the question from many of you. Hopefully, a little. Others asked how I was going to address what's happening in our literary world and our wider world. Especially after the horrendous mass shooting at the Pulse nightclub in Orlando, Florida.

Initially I was going to explore the topic of the future of our gay culture in the face of assimilation. I've been exploring that topic in print for a while now. But following the massacre at Pulse and the amazing writing that has been done in print and all over the Internet to put the events in perspective, I wondered how my concerns about the future of gay culture would mesh with our concerns about the future of gay life altogether in this country.

After the marriage equality vote by the Supreme Court on June 26, 2015, we had a wild honeymoon period in every sense of the word *honeymoon*. What a high it was!

But less than a year later we saw the rise of Trump, the North Carolina bathroom bullshit, the odious religious freedom bills ... and then Orlando. Once again, many of us were reminded that marriage equality and legislative gains are nothing if we fear for our actual safety.

I started thinking about this presentation many months ago, to talk about the preservation of our gay culture. But as I thought about the past and what will come in the future, the present was tumbling out of control.

It became clear to me that if we wanted to be sure we could preserve our gay culture in a changing world, we had to first react to the present—the way we always have—by writing about it.

Throughout the long and often painful journey for our civil rights, it's been writers who have saved themselves and others by writing our stories.

This is illustrated by the fine writing of LGBT reporters and columnists reacting to Orlando. Many writers published blogs, articles, and social media posts that helped us all through the days and weeks that followed the tragedy and the incendiary rise of the political far right.

And throughout history, our writers have taken on this role. They introduced readers to lesbian lives through journalism, non-fiction, fiction and poetry. I don't know how to break it to youngsters, but lesbian literature did not start with Xena fanfic.

Our foremothers expanded, encouraged, and often spurred on the activism and passion that led to gay rights progress. Our written word has been our gay rights archive.

But there's been a lot of talk lately about our gay culture and concern that we might lose it by gaining our rights and disappearing into the swiftly moving mainstream.

We're losing our lesbian bars. Gay newspapers are shrinking. The less we need our special places, the less of them there will be. Some call it progress. I call it a problem.

I want us all to help preserve our special culture: From *Rubyfruit Jungle* to Billie Jean King, drag kings, Harvey Milk, P-town. Our history, our heroes, our catch-phrases. We need to protect them and pass them on.

Gay people have long had secret signs and a shared gay sensibility that, in the past, and still in some places today, allowed a closeted gay community to thrive even as the heterosexual majority despised and discriminated against us.

But as we gain our rights, are we on the brink of making our own culture extinct? We need our rights but we don't want to be dinosaurs.

Travel back. For the boys, in the 1960s, the very act of showing up at a Judy Garland concert and seeing other gay men around the room, all sharing Judy's music and vulnerability, made that denigrated community feel less alone. They didn't even necessarily talk to each other. They just shared the glow and it was often enough.

And in the '50s and '60s, how many lesbians found each other playing half-court basketball, attracted to each other despite wearing those lovely gym suits? Did you wear one???

Lesbian culture has its own jokes, etiquette, magazines and buzzwords. It really hit home to me, traveling with my show. As we become more and more assimilated into society at large, how the heck do we rescue and perpetuate this culture? How does it get handed down?

Not at the bio family dinner table. In most cultures, that's the job of parents, grandparents, and aunts and uncles. My family taught me about chopped liver, matzo ball soup, and the power of Jewish guilt. It wasn't religion, it was culture. What special cultural touchstones did your ethnic families of origin hand down?

How many of us went into professions influenced by our families, as we were schooled in theater, music and art culture, law enforcement culture, health care culture, sports, business, and more? We learned from our tribal elders.

Which begs the question, how the heck are we going to make sure our lesbian culture gets passed down if our alphabet generations do not, for the most part, come from LGBT parents?

You know the answer. It's our job. All of us. It's up to us. We have to remember all that came before and pass it on, or, for younger lesbians, read up on the past and hand it down.

We've each got to be an LGBT storehouse, library, great big oral history of lesbian knowledge, trivia, and even jokes.

How many lesbians does it take to change a light bulb?

Six. One to change the bulb and five to sit around and process. (*rim shot sound effect*)

How many lesbians does it take to change a light bulb?

Six. One to change the bulb and five to organize the potluck. (*rim shot sound effect*)

You know, they say lesbians have no sense of humor. **How many lesbians does it take to change a light bulb?** That's not funny! (*horn*)

But what is funny is a coffee table book that was published over a decade ago, called *When I Knew*. It asked the question "When did you know you were gay?"

One lesbian reported watching Julie Andrews in *The Sound of Music* and wanting to be Christopher Plummer. She made her mother take her back to the movie several times. She said that her mother was happy to do it since she assumed her daughter wanted to be a nun, not that she wanted to sleep with a nun.

One gay man said, "My father was watching the news and they reported that Judy Garland had died. I fainted. I was nine."

When did you know? My parents should have suspected when I was five and had a Halloween meltdown, kicking the Dale Evans fringed cowgirl skirt across the room and demanding a Roy Rogers cowboy hat and six-gun. We need to collect and tell these stories.

After all, we certainly have amazing recordable stories right here in this room. And how about our literary touchstones— *Lesbian Nuns: Breaking Silence, Curious Wine, Above All Honor, The Swashbuckler,* the Jane Lawless books, *Love in the Balance, Beebo Brinker,* and so many more.

They are not just titles and words, they are us. So okay, so what's the game plan for saving our culture?

First, we have to embrace our pioneers and remember how visible they were. Even at a dangerous time for lesbians, separatists like the Gutter Dykes in Berkeley, Radicalesbians in New York, and the famously named Clit Collective food co-op, also in New York. They were *out* and outspoken.

In 1972 in Washington, D.C., the Furies, a separatist, feminist-lesbian collective, formed a residential and work compound with 12 founding Furies who were anti-sexism, anti-patriarchy, and anti-capitalism. Their philosophy was, and I quote, "lesbians have been fucked over all our lives by a system which is based on the domination of men over women." Can't argue with that.

I love that when the group set out to find new members, they recruited at softball games.

But just this past May, the National Park Service added The

Furies' 11th Street SE townhouse to its National Register of Historic Places. It's the country's first lesbian landmark to receive that designation.

Have you heard of The Van Dykes? They were a roving band of van-driving lesbian vegans who shaved their heads, didn't speak to men unless they were waiters or mechanics, and lived along the highways for several years, stopping only on "Women's Land." From the '70s on there was Women's Land all over the United States and Canada—places owned by women where all women, and only women, were welcome.

"Only women—womyn—on the land!" was the battle cry.

We were outlaws forming a culture that was both watchful and outrageous. We had an underground community dedicated to good times in spite of the danger.

And some of the most life-giving, life-saving cultural benchmarks we had were our fledgling publishing houses and late, great feminist bookstores. Only a precious few still exist.

Stories of these cultural flashpoints must be celebrated and handed down to our youngsters.

A Woman's Place in San Francisco, BookWoman in Austin, the Toronto Women's Bookstore, and Old Wives' Tales in San Francisco. There were so many!

They hosted bulletin boards announcing the formation of collectives, phone numbers for therapists, tarot card readers, and cat-sitters. They were community centers. They were lifesavers.

From the 1970s through the 1990s more than one hundred feminist bookstores were alive and trying to stay well. Most succumbed. We have to celebrate their history so they can live on. And our culture can thrive.

Okay, here's an easy cultural quiz. *(theme from Jeopardy)*

The first one is a gimme.

Q: What is the name of the bar in New York's Greenwich Village where the gay rights revolution was said to begin in 1969?

A: The Stonewall Inn. Meanwhile, I was just there and there's still dust from 1969 on the windowsills. Good thing it's dark inside.

Q: What is the name of the first U.S. grassroots lesbian civil and political rights organization, organized in 1955?

A: The Daughters of Bilitis. Tell me the truth; doesn't *Bilitis* sound like a disease? I'm being tested for Bilitis! Actually the name came from a fictional character said to be the BFF of the poet Sappho on the Isle of Lesbos in Greece. When they incorporated in 1957, organizers said their charter description was so vague it could have been a cat-lovers organization. Lesbians—cat rescue . . . same, same!

Q: What was the publication of the Daughters of Bilitis called?

A: *The Ladder*. Many of you already know that some of our most notable pioneering lesbian writers got their start in that publication, delivered to subscribers in a plain brown wrapper. *The Ladder* was the very first communication of any kind sent to a scattered and mostly isolated population of lesbians all over the country.

Q: What was the first novel in the English language recognized as having a lesbian theme?

A: Radclyffe Hall's *The Well of Loneliness*, published in 1928 and found obscene by the British Court for defending "unnatural practices between women." Let's hear it for unnatural practices!!!!

Q: What is the name of the event often called "the original women's Woodstock" and when and where was it held?

A: Michigan Womyn's Music Festival in Oceana County Michigan. 1976-2015. It is fondly recalled as a time when women got naked in the woods. Hence, I never attended. Oh, it wasn't the getting naked that bothered me. It was the woods. Not enough bug spray in the world for this New Yorker.

Q: Can you name the shoe style that caused a rash of lesbian broken ankles in the 1990s?

A: Doc Martens. Nobody needed ankle weights. And it was impossible to sneak up on anybody. *(rim shot)*

Q: Can you name five must-see lesbian films over the past 35 years?

A: Here are my favorites: *Desert Hearts, Tipping the Velvet, The Kids are All Right, Bound, The Hours.*

There were self-loathing ones like *Personal Best* and *Chasing Amy*, fun ones like *Itty Bitty Titty Committee*.

There are at least 40 available on Netflix right now and we must keep them circulating. Let's rewatch all these great and not-so-great films and keep passing our culture along!

Q: What was the name of the reporter purported to have had a long-term lesbian relationship with First Lady Eleanor Roosevelt? Do you know the name of the home they shared?

A: Lorena Hickok. Val-Kill. In Upstate New York. And if you visit, there are not so subtle signs that both women shared that home; although the docents are careful not to mention it, even when somebody like me drove them bonkers with questions. I'm lucky I wasn't thrown out.

Q: Who wrote, *Odd Girls and Twilight Lovers: A History of Lesbian Life in the 20th Century?*

A: Scholar Lillian Faderman. Now, she has a fantastic history herself; check it out.

Q: And finally, what's the name of an unfortunate 1980s lesbian hairstyle?

A: Ahhh, "The Mullet." It always gets a laugh. I have nothing else to say about that, except that it is indeed part of our culture.

We've been able to talk about these things out loud and proud for less than 40 years. So ask yourself, think back. Who are your icons??? Whose legacy do you want to pass along? I know there are icons right here in this room with us. So many people crossed my path who I credit with pushing me to be out and proud. I'll talk about just two.

First, Barbara Gittings.

For people who've paid even the slightest bit of attention to the struggle for gay rights in this country, you probably know the name Barbara Gittings.

If not the name, I bet you've seen the grainy black and white photos, from 1965, in front of the White House, men in suits and ties, women in shirtwaist dresses, raising placards and advocating for gay rights. Barbara Gittings was there, and she called it picketing. Most people call it the very beginning of the entire gay rights movement in this country.

I only got to meet Barbara twice, the second time being a total immersion weekend.

In 2006, Delaware Stonewall Democrats wanted to honor Barbara Gittings. We heard she wasn't in the best of health, having fought cancer for years, and recently undergoing more chemo. She told Stonewall organizers she was hesitant to make the drive to the beach from her home in Wilmington, Delaware, as her partner Kay had mobility issues and wouldn't be coming along. Bonnie and I volunteered to pick Barbara up on Friday night, drive her to Rehoboth, and welcome her to our guest room.

From the minute she hopped, literally, into our car, this petite and lively woman with the delightful smile started peppering us with questions. She wanted to know where we lived, how we met, what movies we liked, the last book we read, how many siblings we had, if we were out of the closet to relatives. It was dizzying. In a happy barrage we answered, exchanged a lot of laughs, and heard a little of her life story, about she and Kay making do with low-paying administrative jobs so they had time to do their real jobs as gay rights activists. Two hours later, when our car turned into our driveway, we were like old friends.

Barbara cautioned that she tired easily and might not be up for too busy a weekend. No problem, we said, our house is yours for resting, relaxing, and whatever you need.

Her next words were, "Where's the best place for dinner? I love great restaurants. And can I meet some of your friends? Please?"

While she disappeared to change clothes, we called four friends to come over for pre-dinner cocktails. When Barbara reappeared, she was wearing white tennis shorts, sneakers, and a bright orange T-shirt with the slogan "Gay? Fine by Me!" on it.

Our friends arrived and Barbara sat cross-legged on our sofa and started to talk ... She described those White House pickets and how she insisted they had to dress conservatively. She talked about the early days of the Daughters of Bilitis, when she was editor of *The Ladder*. We learned the inside story of her arranging for a gay psychiatrist, disguised to protect his identity, coming to speak at the National Psychiatric Association.

That event led directly to the 1973 APA vote to remove homosexuality from their list of mental illnesses. Always going for the impact, she and Kay organized a Kiss-a-homosexual" booth at an American Library Association conference in the 1970s. She got their attention!

We heard more stories at dinner and agreed to Barbara's request to walk the boardwalk. Heading down the one-mile stretch, she walked as fast as she talked, stopping only for salt water taffy and caramel corn. On the return mile I was huffing and puffing to keep up.

The next day, Barbara was up early so she could visit the remaining gay bookstore in town and our LGBT community center. Her energy never flagged as we did the town, came home to change for the Stonewall event, and headed right back out.

It was a perfect summer evening with a large crowd. After an introduction that lauded many of her selfless gay rights activities, Stonewall presented Barbara with a lovely inscribed glass bowl, which she excitedly held over her head for all to see as she gave an impassioned and rousing speech and challenged us to keep up the fight for our rights.

Then it was off to dinner again, and more conversation about iconic events, described by somebody who was actually there.

As we drove her home Sunday, Barbara wanted still more details of our lives and personal history. When we dropped her off, we felt like we'd made a wonderful new friend. We promised to stay in touch and exchanged several emails over the next months. I was totally stunned and saddened a short time later when I heard she had passed away, with Kay at her side. She was only seventy-three.

I'll always have the memory of her charging in and out of our house, curly gray hair askew, asking questions, laughing out loud, and wearing her "Gay? Fine by Me!" T-shirt.

And it's fine by a whole lot of people thanks to Barbara Gittings. Anybody here have the guts to set up a Kiss-a Lesbian Booth here in the hotel lobby? (I figured.)

My second most unforgettable character with a prominent place in lesbian culture was, as you might expect, 2006 Trailblazer Award winner Sarah Aldridge, Anyda Marchant's made-up pen name. She thought it sounded vaguely British and slightly aristocratic.

Anyda was born in 1911 and became a lawyer in 1933 only because she got a scholarship to law school. But what she really wanted to do was be a novelist.

It wasn't until 1972, in her sixties, when she retired from her huge job as a lead attorney for the World Bank, that she finally became novelist Sarah Aldridge.

She and Muriel joined up with Barbara Grier and her partner, Donna McBride, and in 1973 the courageous quartet founded Naiad Press. It was launched in 1974 with the publication of that first Sarah Aldridge novel, *The Latecomer*. The book was a slight, sweet, very old-fashioned romance, but entirely cutting edge as it was the first published lesbian romance with a happy ending. Before that, one lover in any lesbian story had to be thrown under the bus or killed off in some disgusting way. Morality had to triumph.

While the simple Sarah Aldridge tales have been eclipsed today by amazing contemporary stories and diverse storytelling, the early Sarah Aldridge books gave so many lesbians their very first look at themselves on the printed page. They'd lived in a world where they had never read a story featuring the feelings they felt, the impulses they recognized. It was historic.

We are so lucky today, to have all of you in this room, writing and reading about lesbian relationships. But imagine opening a brown paper wrapper on a book that, for the first time ever, reflected your own feelings. What was your first book like that?

But back then, Naiad Press had a tough time. Printers refused to print such so-called filth. A printer would agree, then back out. Imagine the courage it took to hand over that lesbian love story to an ink-covered print shop owner and wait for the disgusted rejection. Sometimes it was just a "no." Sometimes it was a barrage of hatred, sometimes it was a threat to call the police. It took them a year to find a print shop that would print their first book, and even then it had to be secretive. The printer's largest client was a Baptist church. It was a freaky combination.

But through the courage and perseverance of the publishers of Naiad, plus the growing network of gay newspapers and feminist bookstores, the press became, in its day, the most successful lesbian publishing house in the country, perhaps the world.

After Anyda's eleventh novel, she and Muriel withdrew from Naiad and started A&M Books of Rehoboth.

Anyda's fourteenth and final novel was published in 2003 when the novelist was ninety-two years old. She was as giddy with glee as a teenager when her new book arrived from the printer.

When Anyda and Muriel first moved to Rehoboth Beach in the 1950s, they were deeply closeted and silent about their relationship. They stayed that way even as they were publishing those scandalous lesbian books with Naiad.

In fact, Muriel couldn't even say the word lesbian so she coined a new one. When they would see a female couple walking down the street Muriel would say "Shhhh . . ." Eventually, they began to call their own kind *Shushes.*

In 1948, the year I was born, Anyda became one of the first female attorneys at a prestigious D.C. law firm. She met Muriel there. She told me she looked at Muriel one day, and thought "That's *it.*" Although she didn't have any words for what *it* was. Think about it. 1948—before any public respect for, or even acknowledgement of same-sex relationships. Theirs was a bold, courageous and willful choice.

They became feminists almost before the term came into use. Anyda and Muriel hosted Delaware's first-ever National Organization for Women meeting. Anyda described the women having to sneak out of their homes because their husbands were angry about their going to a feminist event. Some of those husbands actually lurked in the street outside, behind trees, to see which Rehoboth women had the nerve to defy them. Anyda phoned the newspaper to get photos of the men hiding in the bushes.

By the turn of the millennium the ladies were aging, although Anyda was still bossy and imperious and Muriel mischievously liked to kiss the young lesbians who came to call—you know, young lesbians, those of us in our 50s and 60s. Once in a while, she'd lean forward in her recliner and pat Bonnie on the behind as she passed by, then look at me, put a finger up to her lips, and giggle.

At one point I was directing a local production of *The Vagina Monologues*. Anyda and Muriel wanted to attend, but a night out at the theatre was too much for them.

So we brought a dress rehearsal to their living room.

Everything was going along fine until one of the actresses came to those famous lines, "Cunt. There I said it. Cunt. Cunt. Cunt."

The actress looked at the elderly audience of two and sputtered "Cu . . . Cuuu . . ." She couldn't do it. Forget the entire point of Eve Ensler's groundbreaking work, these women might have been her grandmothers and she just couldn't.

At which point Anyda leaned forward and said, "Really my dear, you can say it. Naiad Press once published *The Cunt Coloring Book*. We're really rather well aware of the word."

By 2005, the ladies were frail and elderly. But still hosting cocktail salons on their porch. They were Rehoboth's Gertrude Stein and Alice B. Toklas.

By Christmas 2005, Anyda was home, having been diagnosed with a fast-growing cancer and refusing treatment. "I'm almost 95," she said. "There will be no treatment!"

From a hospital bed in the living room she insisted that the frame of the bed be tilted at the perfect angle so she could see Muriel in her chair in the sunroom and call, "Yoohoo, Sweetie" and wave.

Although she was absolutely furious at her deteriorating condition, she continued to rule the roost, giving orders to hospice staff, requesting not just tea, but Prince of Wales tea, discussing newspaper headlines, and demanding her 5 p.m. glass of Dewar's.

The parade of visitors spoke to Anyda and Muriel's vast circle of loving friends. Until almost the last, Anyda would remind me not to make Muriel's drink too strong. And Muriel would hold the glass up to the light and complain that the liquid looked awfully pale.

As Anyda rested one day I read her a letter from a woman named Carol Seajay—former editor of the *Feminist Bookstore News* and an important part of our lesbian publishing culture.

In part, the letter read: "Anyda, it was your vision of a possible world in your first lesbian novel and your vision that we could have such books, and your vision and skills that launched our first, grand lesbian publishing house—and published books that have gone out all over the world, changed countless women's lives, giving hope and opening doors. Yours was an awesome body of work and I hope you are fiercely proud of it all."

Oh, she was.

One day, very near the end, as Anyda napped, Muriel, Bonnie, and I sat discussing the merits of Dewar's vs. Johnny Walker Scotch. Although she had already been quite removed from any conversation around her for a day or two, as we continued the comparison, Anyda sat bolt upright, looked at us with authority, and announced, "The virtue of Johnny Walker is that it can be found all over the globe."

As it turned out, those were her last words. Kind of appropriate.

And as I carried on the work of A&M Books, I have tried, as best I could, to live up to Anyda and Muriel's example ... in both publishing and cocktails.

But frankly my biggest and most iconic inspirations in this world of lesbian literature and culture are all of you. And you don't have it easy, either. While the proliferation of lesbian publishing houses and authors has been astounding and wonderful, the publishing world we now inhabit is nuts.

You have to have the hide of an elephant to look yourself up

191

on Amazon. There, a herd of entrepreneurs are reselling our books. There are used copies selling at fire sale for $1.96, or else a colossal $27.99 as signed collectibles. Just put me on a shelf with the Hummels and Lladros.

Between book piracy, Amazon's price wars, the death of our bookstores, and disappearing LGBT publications, you are all my heroes.

And a sense of humor is mandatory.

Which brings me back to the traditional gay sensibility and our rich history of lesbian books and culture.

Are we up for the challenge of passing it along? Of course we are!

I'm convinced that more than most people, gay people have a wonderful and enduring spirit of adventure, well past senior-hood and into old age, just like Barbara Gittings and Anyda Marchant.

My wife celebrated her 60th birthday on a zip line, and in three weeks we're headed to Iceland to drive around the entire country in an RV. I recently tried riding a Segway and I heard a flapping sound. I think it was my three chins. I kayak with alli-gators, and I made my stage debut after I got my Medicare card.

And from all the stories I've already heard at this conference, we're all in shape to do the hard work of passing along our culture.

Come with me on the adventure; let's commit ourselves to what I call "EduGAYtion." Take a baby dyke to lunch. Join a PFLAG chapter and tell your stories. Host a movie night for younger lesbians so they can enjoy *Desert Hearts*. Give gifts of used books to kids who will love them!

Invite your elders to dinner and ask about the outlaw days. Make an intergenerational connection in a group like a gay chorus or book club.

If your knees won't let you play softball or pickleball, be a scorekeeper or manage a team. And, of course, keep writing and reading like mad women. Shout it out. Read, read, read gay his-tory, gay historical fiction, gay mysteries, romance and the lot.

And revel in Pride. Don't say we don't need parades anymore; we need them more than ever and we should take part. Wear the rainbow, fly the flag, be brave, be visible, celebrate Pride, call out prejudice, and keep nurturing our culture. We owe it to those who follow.

And I leave you with the following advice that has become my motto:

May you all live so fully that the Westboro Baptist Church pickets your funerals.

Thanks for listening! (*rim shot*)

July 2016

Pretty much everybody has written just about everything there is to say about the 2016 Democratic Convention. From Hillary's amazing speech to her bold choice of a white pantsuit, from awesome Sarah McBride, the first transgender speaker at a national political convention, to the hammering home of the "Stronger Together" theme.

For LGBTQ (I'm starting to add *Q* now, but enough, please) people, and our wonderful allies, the Democratic Convention was a history-making, glass-ceiling shattering, spectacularly inclusive affair.

But for me, there was one teeny-weeny special moment, probably thirty seconds or less, that saw me burst into tears. It could have happened as I heard any number of truly moving stories, pleas to end gun violence, warnings about demagogues, and appeals for kindness and caring. Those moments touched me, moved me, made me cheer. Perhaps a tear or two welled up.

But, no, the only moment when I completely lost it was seeing Tyne Daly and Sharon Gless, TV's *Cagney and Lacey*, reunited and singing "What the World Needs Now" with a host of other performers. Bizarre? I thought so.

But then I realized that the seven-year duration of the well-written, groundbreaking female cop buddy show mirrored the most formative time in my life. It premiered on March 25, 1982, just two nights before I met my wife Bonnie.

And yes, I know, Meg Foster was the original Christine Cagney, with Gless picking up in Season Two. But for me, Gless and Daly epitomized strong, independent women with careers, decisions to make, and mostly real-life problems to navigate. In contrast to the married Mary Beth Lacey, Christine Cagney was single and facing many of the issues I faced as an unmarried woman, on my own, learning to deal with a job, a secret, and often discrimination.

Of course, Cagney was not a lesbian in the show. She couldn't have been in 1982, even if the writers wanted her to be, which they didn't. But we could somehow see ourselves in her swagger and her struggles.

It was the closest we'd get for years, unless you count Cher's character in 1983's *Silkwood*, reading Katherine Forrest's *Curious Wine* (also 1983), or the premiere of *Desert Hearts* in 1985. And face it, Sharon Gless was easy on the eyes. And somehow we got a vibe that she was an ally—played out years later by her taking a role as the PFLAG Mom in *Queer as Folk*, and making the sweet 2009 film *Hannah Free*.

Cagney and Lacey enchanted me so much I dabbled in fanfic before I ever knew such a writing genre existed. But I didn't just write my own *Cagney and Lacey* story in honor of the show. I actually worked on a teleplay—a script—and submitted it to the producers. I'd never written a script before, and I really didn't know what I was doing but I threw myself into the breach as only an enthusiastic young person would.

My script saw a policewoman injured on the job and detailed how the show's characters, from the two principals to the other squad members, Lacey's husband, and others, reacted to the surprising news that the next of kin they had to contact was another woman. It wrapped up, mostly happily, and there were rocky moments in the squad room, as it reflected our lives in the mid-1980s.

One night, several months after I forwarded the script to Hollywood, I got a phone call. It came in at 10:30 at night Eastern Standard Time from a young-sounding guy working production on the show. After establishing I was the writer, he made sure to let me know, emphatically, that he had not read the script, as "we're not allowed to read it until it's been through legal."

He told me my script was in the wrong format, and he was going to send me a sample copy of a script so I could redo it correctly.

"And then we can read it," he said, "because it has to go through the lawyers first," we said in unison.

By the following week I received a large packet from the studio with two sample scripts, writing guidelines, paperwork to fill out for their lawyers, and a whole bunch of other stuff. Yes, Bonnie and I concluded it was a lot of trouble to go to for a script nobody had read.

Well here's the upshot: I took my mess of a script, redid it to format, and mailed it off to the infamous lawyers. That same young man and I talked a couple of times after that, and our last call determined that the script would be put on the schedule for the following season of *Cagney and Lacey*. Woo-hoo!

Then the show got cancelled. Major bummer.

But I assure you, my bursting into tears at seeing those icons of mine almost thirty years later at the Democratic Convention had nothing to do with the loss of a writing credit or paycheck (although that would have been nice!) It had everything to do with the many years I traveled vicariously with those women and their TV family as I came out, grew up, and settled down.

By 1988 when the show ended, I was forty. Bonnie and I were suburban homeowners, and we had been living in unmarried bliss for six years and counting. Frankly, by that point I was more like the married Mary Beth Lacey than the single and loving it Christine Cagney.

We had to wait until our 30th anniversary to get married legally, but we finally made it. And now, as retirees and Medicare recipients, we look back so fondly on those *Cagney and Lacey* days. That old script is still in the desk drawer. A lot has changed in 30 years and it would need a hell of a lot of re-writing to reflect changes in attitudes . . . or would it? Maybe I can rework it for *NCIS New Orleans*. As for Ms. Cagney and Mrs. Lacey, I loved seeing "them" standing up for our values.

I never thought I'd have to buy another bright orange string trimmer. I was wrong.

This led me to realize I can calculate my life stages by the kinds of items I have purchased, over and over, through the years.

In our current community of manufactured homes, management mows our lawn, but not, alas, along the fence or inside the postage-stamp yard. We felt sure we could edge the fence and manage the small plot of interior grass with a trimmer, but the machine gagged on the task and died.

I gagged at the thought of buying yet another string trimmer, not to mention a small electric lawn mower. I had sworn those days were behind me. But no, it was déjà vu, as 35 years ago I purchased an electric mower. That was in the "Getting to Know You" stage, when my mate and I were setting up housekeeping.

And the townhouse yard was almost as tiny as the current splotch of green stuff. It turned out to be just a matter of time before my spouse ran over the electric cord with the mower blades, committing Mowercide.

Cordless battery mowers wouldn't be invented for another quarter century so we got a gas mower. Readystart buttons hadn't been invented yet either so we both have residual rotator cuff issues from years of yanking the ornery pull cord.

Joining that expensive gas mower was our first hot tub. It was a splendid wooden barrel tub, a do-it-yourself kit, which seated eight people sitting upright with their legs dangling into the deep foot-well. We hosted lots of backyard parties, which, in turn, led to the purchase of our first charcoal barbecue grill.

Then, entering our 40s, came the Nesting Stage. We upgraded our residence to a single-family home, but still relied on friends to help us move—so we let the hideously heavy hot tub convey with the townhouse, but took the mower and grill along. Within weeks we were worn out from shoving that mower across the much larger lawn. And we didn't even have a hot tub to soothe our weary bones. So in addition to upgrading to a self-propelled mower, we went hot tub hunting.

The safari took us to a fairgrounds hot tub expo, where we fell victim to, I mean invested in, a massive six-person acrylic square, with a dozen air jets and room to host an orca. But not until we had six adults in the thing did we realize we'd all have to be nearly prone with our dozen legs intertwined just to stay submerged. So it became a hot tub for two, three if it was family.

And lo and behold, charcoal was passé so we traded up for a gas grill. In those days they did not come assembled. We bought it at nine in the morning and by 8 p.m. we were still squatting on the deck (the second deck to be built by us, by the way) amid more remaining screws and bolts than you'd need to build the Batmobile. We ordered pizza delivery and froze the ribs.

A word about grill covers: Missing. Every time we had a windstorm our grill cover of the moment would fly into orbit. Had we attached our names, I'm sure one of those black shrouds will eventually be discovered on Mars.

By the time we moved to Rehoboth almost 20 years ago now, we were into the Exhaustion Stage—tired of commuting between two residences and ready for life full-time at the beach. Mayflower Movers schlepped that aging hot tub along to put on the third deck we had to build. We also moved with our third or fourth gas mower, sixth or seventh gas string trimmer and new and improved gas grill. The whole business gave me gas.

Can you guess what happened next? In Rehoboth we had three-quarters of an acre. Yup, enter our pet riding mower. What fun! But sadly, one day, returning from the mower sharpener, we glanced in our rearview mirror and saw our prized mower lurch backward, then roll, in slo-mo, out of the truck.

Everybody thought somebody else had tied it down. The behemoth landed on all fours, wheels splayed, tires going east and west, hood cracked and several of its vital organs hemorrhaging fluids. Ultimately, it got fixed so it could mow, but cosmetically it never recovered.

And in that house, for the next 11 years, between work and volunteering and being out and about, we didn't have much time or inclination to use the hot tub. Cover on, it became an excellent buffet table, used in concert with our new, state-of-the-art, super-duper gas grill with two side burners, a side table, and everything but the kitchen sink. We didn't have time or inclination to mow either, so we hired somebody with their own riding mower and yard-saled both the mower and the hot tub.

In September 2013 we moved to our manufactured home with its teeny yard. Yay, no room for a deck! We're retired now, Happiness Stage, but surprisingly back to mowing by ourselves with the new electric mower and new battery-operated string trimmer. We're holding a lottery to see how long it will be before I run over the lawnmower cord.

Our cumbersome, aging grill, with its never-used side burners, was tossed pretty violently in a recent wind storm and the rusted insides just crumbled. We replaced it with the simplest, cheapest, most utilitarian version we could find, no grill cover/mainsail needed.

And a short time ago we came into possession of an inexpensive, inflatable hot tub for two. We pumped it up and we're in business. It uses regular house power, has a bubbler more powerful than the two costly tubs we previously owned and is perfect for our backyard oasis. Heavenly.

Everything old is new again. Except for us, of course.

August 2016

BOTTOMS UP ... OR SKOL!

As you read this I am doing my final packing for a trip to Iceland.

Bonnie has always wanted to go there and she's infected me with the wanderlust, too. So in the midst of the scalding weather I'm packing sweaters, turtlenecks, waterproof socks, hiking boots, pants that zip off to become shorts (in case of a rare heat wave), and an opaque eye mask for sleep, as we should expect only two or three hours of darkness this time of year.

We're taking electricity converters for our gadgets, camera and my phone, which, alas, will have to suffice as my computer, plus a bag of guidebooks and maps. I expect that my column about our experiences will be thumbed on my phone.

It's going to be an adventure! Especially since we will spend the 10-day trip traveling around the entire island nation of Iceland in a small recreational vehicle. Ah, you know we love a land yacht. But this was not our initial thought. However, research revealed that 10 days in a rental RV was about half the price of 10 nights in a hotel plus rental car.

It was a no-brainer, especially since we adore traveling by RV and Iceland is noted for its RV culture. You can stop and stay anywhere—tourist sites, in cities, on farms and, of course, numerous RV parks. Sounded like fun to us.

We are set to travel to the land of glaciers, volcanoes, geothermal soaking pools, waterfalls, ice caves, puffins, whales, herring, and fish soup. Oh, and geysers, which they pronounce *geezers*, which prompts me to ask what we old people are called.

But here's the scary thing about our 10 days on the road. I have reluctantly agreed that except for our first night in Reykjavik (and I will explain this in a moment), we will make no advance reservations or plans to stay in particular places. This consummate, (some would say pathological) planner will be flying by the seat of her pants, without a net. Wherever the trip takes us. *Yikes!* Yes, I have packed my anti-anxiety drugs.

I'll let you know if we wind up sharing quarters with chickens, goats, or Icelandic Trolls (a thing, apparently). About the Icelandic language: challenging! Fortunately, almost everyone in Iceland speaks English. But as in all countries, the natives appreciate foreigners making an attempt at speaking the local tongue. We will try, but it's going to be crazy. From the Seljalandsfoss Waterfall and Kirkjubaejarklaustur town to the Snaefellsnes Peninsula and Upper Borgarfjordur, we're in trouble.

Maybe we should stay only in the towns of Vik and Hofsos just to make it simpler.

Now, about our first night in the capital city of Reykjavik: We fly overnight on August 5, arriving at 6:30 a.m. on August 6—just, by happenstance, hitting the city on the last day of the week-long 2016 Iceland Pride Celebration. We'll be in time to attend the big parade. And it is big. In 2014, over 90,000 people (one quarter of the country's population, by the way) came to celebrate and catch the carnival-like festivities.

So we figured we should drop our bags at a hotel, get in on the Pride events, watch the parade, and then crash for a night's sleep before setting out on the Ring Road in our rented RV. From the renowned Blue Lagoon to the famous fjords, we're hoping for a major adventure.

Iceland's most famous celebrity is the singer Bjork. If not remembered for her music, she is noted for that ridiculous swan dress she wore at the Oscars one year. I prefer to applaud Iceland for electing the world's first female—and first openly gay prime minister, Johanna Siguroardottir, in 2008. Way to go, Iceland.

I'm looking forward to my first sip of Brennivin, Iceland's signature distilled beverage. Bottoms up or Skol!

August 2016

Okay, I'm happy to report I survived my free-range Iceland experience. We did not sleep with chickens (although we had close encounters with sheep), always found a convenient campground, and still prefer vodka to their bitter Icelandic schnapps.

While it was 105 degrees and sizzling in most of the U.S., it was 52 degrees and wet in summery Iceland. And we had about 20 hours of daylight each day to enjoy the weather. What were we thinking?

Actually, the trip was pretty amazing. We traveled around the entire country in a small RV along Iceland's famous Ring Road. When the guidebooks said it was easy, they hadn't imagined my mate re-learning a standard transmission on roads with no shoulders, unless you count a 10-story drop to the sea as a shoulder. We spent a lot of time screaming.

The occasional flimsy guardrail looked like it wouldn't stop a rolling trash can—which, by the way, pretty much described the RV after a week of muddy feet, sodden clothing, and fish sandwiches. My mate did all the driving, as I never did learn to use a clutch and shift for myself. *Badabing!*

If the road wasn't scary enough, you'd see a warning sign with a giant exclamation point and then have no translation of the word under it. "Sheep in the road!" would have been a good guess. Not to mention the frequent one-lane bridges where you'd play Icelandic chicken with the cars coming the other way.

But we saw fjords, volcanoes, lava fields, glaciers, waterfalls, those free-range sheep, puffins, black beaches and icebergs. Ate a lot of fish. Visited unpronounceable places. Loved the people. Soaked in thermal pools, saw a geyser and gawked at fumaroles—rock piles belching stinky, sulphurous steam.

Unlike the U.S. where there would be fences, walls and other impediments to getting up close and personal with the attractions, Iceland trusts its visitors not to do foolish things. Although near the fumaroles burping boiling liquid, there was a small sign noting, "Do not reach for hot water or steam, nearest hospital, 65 kilometers."

I loved those steaming "hot pots" from the geothermal springs below the moonscape terrain, the touristy Blue Lagoon, the friendly people, and marvelous fish and lamb dinners. The ubiquitous waterfalls, lagoons full of blue icebergs, black beaches, whales, and puffins took our breath away.

Much of the country looks like the film set for Matt Damon on Mars. There are no trees except ones people plant on farms and in cities. We were cold and wet while everyone in Rehoboth was boiling and schvitzing.

By week's end, we were mildewing. And don't tell my wife, but I think my camping days are over. Every time I got in or out of the vehicle I sprained myself. The bed was like sleeping on an ironing board, and the bathroom was so small (*How small was it?*) you had to step out to change your mind. *Bada bing.*

The sun didn't set until 10 p.m. and came back up around 5 a.m. Time was told on the military clock so our daily mantra was, "It's 1700 o'clock somewhere."

But if I can share just one trip highlight it would be our arrival in the capital city of Reykjavik on, of all things, Pride Weekend. And holy Donna Summer do they do it right!

Every single store, hotel, and restaurant flew rainbow flags, had rainbow-decorated windows, or had painted (*painted!)* storefronts and sidewalks the full spectrum. Hundreds of lamppost banners celebrated Pride, which had already been going on for days with shows, dances, movies, and more. Then came the parade. Iceland has less than 350,000 people, but at least 75,000 people stood waiting along the route—locals, people from around the country, and lots of international visitors.

It was a human rainbow—gay, straight, many, many families with kids, people of all ages, ethnicities, and style. Youngsters wore rainbow face paint and rainbow clothing, while even some of the public sculptures were festooned with rainbow leis.

Volunteer parade organizers were visible but not plentiful and there was no police presence, as none was needed. It was reassuring that the parade kicked off with Iceland's version of Dykes on Bikes, an honor guard of local officials, backed up by a group from the American Embassy. Then came floats with disco-dancing drag queens, gay bar employees, commercial entities like banks and restaurants, and on and on, all to the soundtracks of "I Will Survive" and "Dancing Queen."

Afterward, we left the Rainbow Gayla and shows to the youngsters and held out in a nearby pub. Everybody partied with pride and an infectious air of unity. So grand, in fact, that I wish our local Pride parades could be like this—everybody from businesses to elected officials all taking part, flying the rainbow and celebrating.

I can dream, can't I?

August 2016

So there we were in Iceland. You know me. Nothing is so bad if it's worth the story you can tell. Well, this last one almost took me out.

One day, despite windy, rainy conditions we showed up at the dock in the town of Husavik, one of the more pronounceable places, to enjoy a four-hour whale watch and puffin hunt.

Already dressed in long johns, quick-dry pants, turtlenecks, sweaters and jackets, we were stuffed and then zipped into bright red, full-body flotation suits. Lurching down the pier and onto the restored wooden sailing vessel I could have passed for the Abominable Snowman.

Taking a seat and hoping not to move for the next half-day, I gazed at our fellow travelers. With everybody zipped up, hooded, and gloved, it was a HazMat team in Ray Bans.

So we sailed toward the Greenland Sea and it's true, Iceland is mostly green and Greenland, they say, is mostly ice. The water was rough, wind biting cold, whales and puffins scarce.

As the boat could only get so close to the puffin-roosting island, the hundreds of white globs on the cliffs, purportedly puffins, could just as easily have been roosting marshmallows.

The boat pitched and rolled as we circled and circled the area, seeking whales. After a while the crew raised the sails and the captain turned off the boat's noisy engine so we could sail round and round in glorious peace and quiet. Unfortunately, it was so quiet we could hear the unmistakable sound of humans at the stern, sending breakfast back to the sea.

After about three frigid, rainy, uneventful hours, with waves sloshing across the deck and hypothermia in the offing, we saw one enormous humpback whale break the surface of the water right smack in front of us. The mighty mammal then took a swooshing dive, displaying her majestic tail as she reentered the water. Really intense.

When a crew member shouted, "Possible whale at starboard!" I raced for a glimpse, skidded across the wet deck, lost my balance and, unable to course correct in my costume, crashed down on the slippery surface like a tree falling in the forest. And yes, if a tree falls and 40 tourists are there to hear the sound, it's still humiliating. I went down hard, on my own majestic tail, flat on my back, arms flailing like an upended tortoise.

I saw my spouse, at least I think it was my spouse, gaping at me, horrified, from above. I don't know whether she feared I was dead, or was frightened it was her job to get me back up. As it happened, it took a village.

Thanks to my 15 layers of protective clothing, all that was seriously hurt was my pride. Then, as if to celebrate the raising of the fallen Yeti, the crew served hot chocolate. While it was a charming touch, I had to wonder what genius decided to disburse fluids to people zipped into onesies who'd been without bathroom access for four hours.

I declined the Swiss Miss and immediately after docking, peeled off my snowsuit and ran for the WC.

And while it was a seriously long, cold and wet slog at sea, at least we got to see one spectacular whale take a dive. The rest of the passengers got value added. Thanks to me, they saw two whales go down.

And by the way, it's amazing how much padding you can wear and still come home with bruises big as softballs. As I have said before, thank goodness it's always 1700 o'clock somewhere.

September 2016

Now before I get in trouble with Pink Iceland, a fantastic LGBT travel organization, let me say I loved Iceland's famous Blue Lagoon and would go back in a minute no matter how much fun I make of it. But there's fun to be made.

Some years ago, upon first hearing about the Blue Lagoon—Iceland's biggest tourist attraction—I couldn't wait to visit this natural phenomenon. It's a swimming lagoon filled with seawater heated to 100 degrees by underground geothermal seismic activity.

Sort of.

When traveling from the airport to Iceland's capital of Reykjavik, we passed a giant geothermal energy plant adjacent to the famous lagoon. How marvelous, I thought, that this natural lagoon, heated by underground thermal energy is able to generate heat and power for an entire capital city!

Yeah. Well, it's the other way around.

Turns out that the bluish water, which indeed comes from geothermal seawater deep in the earth, is what's pumped out of the power plant, creating the Blue Lagoon. And it wasn't until the 1980s, when some public relations genius spied locals bathing in the warm pools caused by the run-off. "Aha!" he thought, "We will make this industrial run-off a massive tourist attraction and turn it into Iceland's Disney World!"

It started with a trickle and one lonely bathhouse. Over the ensuing years, using natural lava rock instead of recognizable pool tiles, entrepreneurs expanded the run-off stream, improved the amenities, and now it's a Shangri-La rising from the moonscape-like rubble that is suburban Reykjavik.

The Lagoon employs hundreds of people in an area that can use employment, and literally thousands of people visit it daily to bathe in the blue water and smear silica (that comes from the water) on their faces. Oh, and they buy beauty products that are beauty byproducts from the minerals in the lagoon.

It makes me darn proud of my public relations profession.

Weeks before we visited, we made reservations. There's the Standard ticket, which buys entry and a silica mud mask; Comfort ticket, adding a towel; Premium ticket (our choice) adding a bathrobe, slippers, drink at the bar and a reservation for dinner complete with a glass of Prosecco. Oh, and an algae mud mask in addition to the silica.

The Luxury package added a host of expensive anti-aging products to take home but failed to include a total face-lift, so we figured it was too late for us and passed on the products.

Fast forward. On Blue Lagoon day, we arrive at the parking lot overflowing with tour buses, in the shadow of the power plant. We join the unwashed masses, chattering in a veritable United Nations of tongues, surging toward the entry.

We are each given a plastic high-tech bracelet, which knows which services we purchased, and gets us through the turnstile, where we pick up our towel, bathrobe and slippers. We move fast as the surging mob behind us threatens to overtake our position.

Rushed off to the ladies lockers, we arrive to find a large flock of naked women, chirping in any number of Asian dialects, Norse, and possibly Pig Latin. Terrified, I hug the wall, mouth agape, clutching my rented robe. Bonnie grabs me, points to a locker and demands I get out of my stupor as well as my clothes and head for the mandatory shower.

On the wall there are explicit directions for what and where to wash and monitors standing by to assure compliance.

"What are these, the orifice police?" I ask as Bonnie shoves me under the showerhead.

And then we all struggle into our bathing suits. Only women can understand the torture of trying to insert a wet body into a dry bathing suit. It's an Olympic trial.

Well suited, we press our high-tech bracelet against the locker to shut it securely and join the now-washed masses heading for the Lagoon.

Ahhhh. I get it. The air is cool at 60 degrees but the water is gloriously warm. And blue. And the lagoon is so big (how big is it?) that the masses disperse, leaving us plenty of privacy as we float and swim and luxuriate in the comforting mineral-infused power plant run-off. Weird.

We swim up to the silica mask kiosk, grab a handful of white goop, and apply it all over our faces. It would have been easier with putty knives. The stuff quickly becomes drying spackle. I smile and a fissure opens along my laugh lines. I laugh because there are hundreds of bright white, spackle-covered faces around me, like a sea of mimes.

We dunk our Kabuki-masked heads under the water's surface to rinse and swim for the bar, where our magic bracelets know we get a complimentary beer. Swimming away, savoring the Icelandic brew, we drink and dive with impunity. It really is glorious.

Then it's back to the kiosk for the algae mask. "It's an anti-aging marvel," says the handsome young man in the kiosk as he offers up the green sludge.

"Too late. That ship has sailed," I say.

"No, look at me," he says, "I'm 75." Good one.

We obediently apply the green algae muck to our noses, cheeks and chins and start singing the score from Wicked. Bonnie channels Kermit singing "It's not easy being green." As for me, I'm Lou Ferrigno's Incredible Hulk.

Green at the gills, we swim behind a waterfall, travel the circumference of the enormous lagoon, and marvel at the natural lava rocks masking its man-madeness. We frolic, luxuriate some more and then, algae mask hardened to perfection, I crack a smile. Literally. Time for dinner and Prosecco.

We wade out of the lagoon, don our terry robes and slippers and trudge back to the lockers. Mercifully, the tour buses have stopped arriving and the changing area is no longer a massive peep show. We scrub the vestiges of green mud from our faces, dress, return our terry cloth and, using our electronic wrist bands, verify that we drank no more than was due us on our prepaid ticket. Then, we use the wristband once more to open a compartment in the exit area, surrender said wristband and watch the turnstile open automatically to let us out. Very high tech, but I was disappointed it didn't have a Rosetta Stone app to help us pronounce "get me a glass of bubbly, stat!"

Frankly, we didn't expect much from a fancy restaurant at a tourist attraction, but we got a great surprise, enjoying delicious arctic char and lamb chops along with that included bubbly.

And we toasted to the marketing and promotional superstars who turned power plant leftovers into one of National Geographic's 25 wonders of the world. It's enough to turn us PR hacks green with envy.

September 2016

Marie Kuda has passed away. The 76-year-old LGBT activist, journalist, essay writer and educator was in a nursing home in her beloved Chicago.

I got the sad news from Tracy Baim, editor of Chicago's *Windy City Times,* a thriving LGBT newspaper in that city.

That the publication is thriving, along with an equally thriving population of LGBT citizens nationwide, is surely due in no small part to the role Kuda (that's how she signed her letters and e-mails) played. She promoted dialogue and understanding between gay men and lesbians, and between the gay community and heterosexual society, in the decades when that was a tough job at best.

Kuda organized five national lesbian writers' conferences and published, in the '70s, the first annotated bibliography cataloguing lesbian literature in *Women Loving Women*; was a member of the Gay and Lesbian Task Force for the American Library Association and was appointed by Chicago's mayor to the city's first Committee on Gay and Lesbian Issues. She was inducted into the first class of Chicago's LGBT Hall of Fame in 1991. Marie Kuda spoke her mind, in print, about discrimination, injustice and the positive attributes of gay, lesbian, and transgender people.

She was a pioneer and a part of our lesbian history that I believe we should celebrate and pass along.

I "met" Kuda by e-mail. After my mentor Anyda Marchant (who wrote under the name Sarah Aldridge) passed away, I wrote to Kuda to let her know.

In return, I got a long, detailed e-mail about the prominent place she thought Anyda should occupy in lesbian history. She emphasized her courage in co-founding Naiad Press, her tenacity in dealing with sometimes difficult colleague Barbara Grier, her willingness to write lesbian romances with happy endings, and then her setting out to make their publication happen.

Kuda and I had a several-month e-mail conversation, much of it discussing Anyda's departure from Naiad Press and the real reasons why. That fascinating tale is for a column coming up shortly in these pages.

For now, let me just say that a true pioneer has left the building.

When I responded to Tracy Baim (who is, like Kuda, a powerful and respected LGBT journalist and historian in Chicago) about Kuda's passing, Tracy answered, "She loved your books. There was one with her in the nursing home."

What a wonderful surprise.

Farewell, Kuda, and thanks for all the remarkable good you have done for us all.

September 2016

Okay, people, listen up. Here comes digital bait. As we surf the web, mean jerks with ugly agendas are tossing online chum to stir us up. We take the bait. It's Internet flotsam and jetsam. Wow, this may be the first time I've managed to embed the name of this column in an actual essay. Cool.

And the flotsam I mean is fake news sites. I'm disgusted at having to consult Snopes.com on a regular basis. You do know Snopes, right? It's an invaluable website, ever on high alert, to debunk all manner of false, bogus, phony internet claims, theories, news stories, and other dangerous jetsam.

I cannot figure out why the icky trolls post this fake stuff to sucker-punch web readers. But they do a frighteningly good job. I guess it's capitalism at play, as we are misled into reading a new conspiracy theory about Princess Diana's death (just a rehash), or the sad truth about Dolly Parton (there was nothing sad to report), and then get bombarded with ads for miracle diets, anti-aging goop, and prepaid burials.

Yes, I can be fooled into clicking this stuff from time to time. Believing it? Not so much.

But thank goodness for Snopes' Field Guide to Fake News Sites and Hoax Purveyors. According to Snopes, "Fake/hoax news sites . . . are an attempt to play on gullible people who do not check sources and will just pass the news on as if it were really true." How that infuriates me. How that amazes me. Are people really that dumb? (Author's note: based on the 2016 Presidential election campaign, I say yes, they are. *Trump*????) But I digress.

In contrast to fake sites, satire websites are sites that make fun of the news. These over-the-top, hilarious stories can be very funny indeed, especially in this hideous election season. But they are satire! The Onion.com is the most brilliant at it. But, sadly, some folks who are humor challenged get buffaloed and pass humor along as truth. Seriously??? You're gonna believe headlines like "Scientists Find Strong Link Between Male Virility, Wearing Mötley Crüe Denim Jacket," or "70% of Trump Endorsements Made after Staring at Ceiling for 4 Hours"?

The Borowitz Report is another brilliant and hilarious satire site written by humorist Andy Borowitz. The fact that the venerable *New Yorker* magazine purchased The Borowitz Report Blog, means that a quick glance at a headline with the attribution "The New Yorker" can cause momentary confusion. But seriously, people, read the story before passing along the headline! Do you really want to be known as somebody who believes "BREAKING: White House Authorizes Search for President's Mojo" is a real headline?

I'm also done with careless readers who don't check dates and sources. At first, even I was caught feeling sad about the death of a celebrity who actually kicked the bucket several years ago. I've seen such "news" circulate on like wildfire, caught hours and hours and hundreds of morose comments later by somebody actually paying attention. "Um, Maya Angelou died in 2014."

I have to admit, the confusion between satire and real current events is not a new phenomenon.

Apparently journalist/humorist Mark Twain wrote hoax news all the time in his hometown newspaper. There are tales of the author fleeing from the authorities over stories he made up. However, the newspaper, at some point, did note that the stories were fake. I see no such disclaimers on fake news dot coms.

And of course, "Woman gives birth to space alien" is supermarket tabloid worthy. I don't think people believe this kind of event is possible, but why do they laugh at it in the grocery store yet find it more credible on the web????

And while respected newspapers print satirical features every April Fool's Day, it seems that online every day is fool's day, as these fake stories proliferate and get passed along.

We must be vigilant. We must parse them all and make sure they are true! Like last week, when I read this headline: "Weasel Shuts Down World's Most Powerful Particle Collider." Ha-ha-ha!!!!

It turned out to be true. Sadly, the weasel did not survive.

Okay, fool me once, shame on me, fool me twice . . . etc. So imagine my skepticism upon reading the headline, "Dr. Heimlich Uses His Maneuver at Retirement Home, Saves 87-Year-Old Woman."

Oh come on! But no, it turned out to be astoundingly true. The 96-year-old physician who invented the punch-in-the-gut move to dislodge food from a choking victim's windpipe actually had a chance to use his own maneuver. I'd say "you can't make this stuff up," but you can. They do it all the time. But this one was true. It's so hard to tell the flotsam from the jetsam.

Which is why I like the nautical definition of the word *flotsam*: anything floating in the water from which there is no response when an offer of a cocktail is made.

There's something I can believe.

October 2016

In an already insane election season, today's news is not even the craziest. But it hits closest to home. Right-wingnut radio host Rush Limbaugh recently started screeching about the rise of lesbian farmers.

And I am one.

You may recall that in the fall of 2014 I discovered a crop of baby pumpkins sprouting in the tiny mulch bed in front of my house. The total crop on my "womyn's land" was three small pumpkins, and I went out of my gourd with glee at being an urban farmer.

Sadly, the pumpkin patch remained fallow in 2015, I hope through no fault of mine. The vines turned to mulch and October bore no fruit. I feared it was the end of my nascent farming career.

But come 2016, along with the autumn equinox, the leafy vines and bright yellow flowers returned, shielding four baby pumpkins, pumpkinettes, really, from the unusually hot late September sun.

Yay! Production was up by 25 percent and I was back working the land.

Imagine my shock when I heard that Limbaugh had discovered a USDA program called "Rural Pride"—started to improve the lives of rural queers living outside metropolitan areas. Limbaugh began shouting that the program was an "attack," orchestrated by the Obama administration, on what he noted was the last conservative bastion—rural America.

Fearing that subsidized lesbian farmers could overrun rural communities, he shouted, "I never knew lesbians wanted to get behind the horse and the plow and start burrowing."

Oh honey, I did. Wearing flannel and waving pitchforks.

The whole thing sounded so incredible to me I checked it out. Even the Internet's hoax patrol Snopes.com confirmed the news.

Calling the meme *Pink Dawn*, Snopes noted that "Conservative radio pundit Rush Limbaugh railed against what he described as an Obama administration plot to pay lesbians to become farmers and invade conservative rural strongholds."

I say, "You go, girls!"

As for me, this New Yorker is about to harvest the cream of the crop (the top of the heap) and celebrate my home on the range.

Cartoon by Rob Waters

October 2016

THE NEWS IS MAKING ME NUTS

Just like everybody else, I'm about to lose my eff-ing mind over U.S. politics. Is America going to hell in a handbasket propelled by Donald Trump, or will Hillary Clinton, a sane and experienced candidate, be elected President of the United States?

This election reminds me of the famous quote by losing candidate Adlai Stevenson, who ran against Dwight Eisenhower in the 1950s. When a constituent said to him, "You're the thinking person's candidate," he replied, "Yes, but I need a majority."

Can there really be a majority of ignorant, racist bigots in this country? Possibly.

And if you need any further evidence, here's what happened to a friend of mine, in her own words from facebook, when she went to vote here at the beach on primary day.

I wish I had gotten a picture of the woman who did not want me to vote today.

I walked in the door. A gentleman said, "Can I help you sir?" I corrected him that I was not a sir. He did not apologize.

I said, "I will go to the other table where they won't insult me."

But the person at table two informed me I was not in that district. The person at table three smiled at me, looked at my voter registration card and she said, "Alicia—that's a pretty name, but that's not you."

"Yes it is," I replied.

She said, "But it's a woman's name."

I said, "Are you questioning if it is me or if I am a woman? I AM a woman."

She then said, "Really?"

I repeated, "Are you questioning if I am a woman?"

"Yes," she said.

"Really?" My anger was rising. I started to gesture taking off my shirt and said, "Would you like proof?"

The police lady standing off to the side steps in. "Can I help you, sir?" I said, "You too?"

Finally, they led me to the sweet lady who signed me in under my registered name and then I voted.

I'm mostly angry by the rudeness and lack of apology by anyone. Is this a case of gender insensitivity or a crude form of voter suppression? Or both?

Well, I say both. The way this election season is going I am absolutely certain it's gender insensitivity. Why? Because a certain orange-faced, comb-overed, megalomaniacal bully has, to bastardize his campaign slogan, " MADE AMERICA HATE AGAIN".

And the haters feel they have the right to say whatever they think, no matter who it hurts. And here's the important thing—while these kinds of confusions do happen, frequently, it's the aftermath here that is so frightening. Nobody felt the need to admit their error and apologize. No one was sorry for offending the voter.

Bigots have been emboldened to make their offensive mistakes (if it was a mistake, hard to know) and then display absolutely no remorse, embarrassment, guilt, no nothing. They have been granted permission to offend, at will, the people they have been encouraged to despise.

Not a pretty picture.

And Alicia, I apologize to you in the name of the assholes who offended you and those who wish to continue doing so.

As for me, I make it a practice not to vote for anybody endorsed by the KKK and the American Nazi Party.

November 9, 2016

Holy hell, President-Elect Trump.

As you read this, many months or even years later, you have some idea of how it all turned out. I hope my worst or even my tiniest fears have not come true.

But it was a bleak day in the United States on November 8, 2016, if you were not a straight, white, Christian person. Oddly, the many women who voted for President-Elect Donald Trump seemed not to feel the target on their backs or the inequality in their paychecks. Eventually, it will dawn on them.

As I sit here writing, I'm angry, sad and scared, with no clue what the future will hold. I'm fried. In the new America, I hope these words won't get me convicted. That Hillary Clinton won the popular vote by millions but will not be president has me becoming uncorked. Some 18th century law rendering my state of Delaware virtually irrelevant is irritating beyond words. So I won't say any more about it.

But I will ask: What kind of country is this? What the hell happened to kindness? Civility? Class?

I do know that this 18-month election season, overflowing with stupidity, bigotry, hatred, and lies was actually a peaceful (so far) ballot box revolution. Like the Arab Spring, it was the American Autumn. People wanted change regardless of the lack of qualifications of the changer. I'm trying to understand.

Clearly, a smidge under half the people in this country (thanks to that obsolete electoral college thing) have mistaken reality shows for reality.

But of all the stupid on display in this election, the most disheartening trend is the nation's willingness to accept outrageous lies as fact. The media doesn't call out the lies or liars and demand retractions; the populace itself doesn't demand a stop to the lying; campaigns and news outlets lie at will and there are no penalties.

There must be consequences for knowingly lying. We must

disprove the lies by the politicians (of both parties), campaigns and the media itself, and liars must be fined, big time. News organizations must be outed and have to pay up. Talking heads must be called to task and required to fork over the big money. Hell, if making money is the motive for repeating the lies on the news, let's hit them where it hurts.

But how?

Listen, merely 20 years ago, people thought it was just fine to let their dogs poop all over sidewalks and lawns without feeling the need to clean it up. Likewise, few people thought twice about driving buzzed or even drunk.

But in the past two decades, our consciousness has been raised about those two issues and others like them. Almost all of us hand over our keys or call Uber when we know we'd be driving impaired.

Likewise, it has become socially unacceptable not to clean up dog poop.

But what about the crap that comes out of our campaigns and the media that report on it? Now it's society's turn to tackle the notion that it's okay to concoct phony political scandals, spread bold-faced lies, and torpedo reputations with outrageous falsehoods.

Guess what? It's not okay. We need to echo those immortal words from the film *Network,* "I'm mad as hell and I'm not going to take it anymore!"

Of course, it would be a lot easier if people's pants actually did burst into flame when they lied or their noses grew into giant dildos when they made stuff up. But alas, not so.

So we need a national, nonpartisan Lie Detection Society, headed by a truthiness czar with a staff of researchers to call out lies and stop the bullshit.

Just as "curb your dog" laws made us scoop the poop and the heroic MADD (Mothers Against Drunk Driving) made it unacceptable to drive drunk, we need a new acronym to take the campaign poop out of politics. Let it be unacceptable or at least very expensive to lie. We can do it. What's a good acronym?

CALL: Citizens against Lying Liars
COLD: Citizens Operating Lie Detectors
CAPP: Citizens Against Prevaricating Politicians
CRAB: Citizens Raging Against Bullshit
CRUD: Citizens Rejecting Utter Deceit
CRAP: Citizens Raging Against Prevaricators

You get the idea. Pick one. Let's organize. I stand ready to work.

YOUR SPINACH IS REPORTING IN

Eventually I had to get up off of the sofa and stop sulking. By the evening of the day after that shocking (to me) election result, the front page of my newspaper slipped to the floor when I left the room. Upon my return I discovered that Windsor had ripped it to shreds. That made me laugh. So I sat down with him on the floor and joined in, ripping up the rest of the newspaper, from the obituaries to the classifieds, laughing and moving on.

And just when I thought it was safe to go back into the water, I got a call from a friend who lurks on the Internet looking for things to warn me about. I learned that now MIT says we have to be careful what we say in front of our spinach.

That's right, scientists are turning spinach into an information-gathering early warning system. According to a press release from MIT, by embedding spinach leaves with something called carbon nanotubes, engineers have turned spinach plants into sensors that can detect bombs and wirelessly tell a smartphone about it.

Seriously? Now I have to worry about calls from vegetables other than telemarketers?

MIT put out a press release calling the program "a novel demonstration of how we have overcome the plant/human communication barrier." Please, spinach and other gassy vegetables have been talking to me for years. But before, when my lunch was repeating, it wasn't repeating what it heard.

We're used to being warned that certain foods or plants are bad for your health, but in a case of "turnabout is fair play," this is the first time foods and plants will be warning us.

As the folks at MIT see it, when chemicals in the groundwater are sucked up naturally by the plant, the newly engineered leaves emit a fluorescent signal. That, in turn, is read with an infrared camera on a smartphone, which then emails the user.

Oh good God, if homeland security gets an urgent email from

its spinach, I pray it doesn't go to junk mail and delay the bomb squad.

Here's a question: If spinach can talk, is it still a vegetable? Can vegans still eat it? It may not have eyes, but now it has ears.

And while we're talking spinach, what else can we expect from this talking spinach? If these plants are turning into snitches, will our spinach rat us out when we go to the fridge for a frozen Snickers instead of a celery stalk? Will broccoli learn the game, become an informant, and report me to my Fitbit?

In fact, we'll have to get rid of the phrase "vegging out." Spinach plants will soon be working as hard as bomb-sniffing Labrador retrievers. The farmer in the dell now listens for spinach chatter and supervises an undercover spy ring.

When James Bond is captured by his nemesis and bomb-sniffing spinach saves the day, is the movie *You Only Diet Twice?* Or *Live and let Diet? Diet Another Day?* You can stop now, Fay.

Wait a minute! Has anybody told Popeye the Sailor Man? If loose lips sink ships, now he's got to forget about Bluto and keep an eye on his spinach. Popeye can still shout, "I yam what I yam," but his spinach can't say the same. Now it's Big Brother.

If you see Rudy Giuliani coming toward you with a spinach toupee, duck and cover.

The possibilities are endless. As long as spinach can reach out and warn someone, what else might it do? Scientists think leafy plants can really get into monitoring the environment while they suck up a lot of information from their surroundings. There are plans to make bionic plants that change color to warn us of things. Beyond our country just going green, we're hoping spinach can go pink or purple to report upcoming droughts, plagues or the zombie apocalypse.

In fact, scientists are also hoping that sensors in other plants, such as the Madagascar periwinkle, which produces drugs to treat cancer, can monitor their own health to maximize the yield of those rare compounds. Wow. I'd try to make a joke about Madagasgar periwinkle, but its name is already funny enough for a listening device. "Come here, Madagasgar periwinkle, I need you!"

So here's the thing. Knowing the potential of spinach to forewarn, I'm planting a crop in my teeny backyard. I'll follow the news from MIT and learn how to use my spinach to its full tattletale potential.

Wikipedia suggests "keeping an eye on your plants and harvesting when the leaves reach desired size. But don't wait too long, as bitterness will set in quickly."

Tell me about it. I'm already bitter that my salad is smarter than I am and apparently far more in demand in the job market. I'll keep you posted on my communication farm.

In the meantime, I've got to go. I hear my spinach calling.

ON THE CORRECT SIDE OF HISTORY

I admit it, I was worried.

I learned last summer that a book, called *Indomitable: The Life of Barbara Grier*, by historian and author Joanne Passet was in the works. Author, publisher and gay rights pioneer, Grier and her partner Donna McBride were two of the founders of the now legendary Naiad Press, along with Anyda Marchant and Muriel Crawford. You've heard from me about Anyda and Muriel for years. And these four women founded the first and arguably most successful lesbian publishing house in the country.

I adored my dear friends Anyda and Muriel, and worried that with two sides to every story and this being a biography of Barbara, the last word on their publishing legacy might be told from Barbara's vantage point alone.

And I had something to worry about since Barbara and Anyda had clashed early and often in the founding and subsequent running of Naiad Press. Their head-butting morphed into a full-blown feud prior to the two-couple business partnership breaking apart for good in 1994.

As for Barbara Grier herself, she was a complicated character. I'd heard much from Anyda and many others about her being needlessly tough on employees, rudely direct in criticism to and about writers and colleagues, and ruthless in business. I'd also heard from Anyda and others that she could be generous to a fault, loyal beyond words, and one of our publishing and lesbian rights heroes. Complex. People loved her or wanted to vilify her, little in between. I wish I had known her for a thousand reasons, but also so I could give you my opinion of this very influential lesbian pioneer.

The instant the book was published this fall, I grabbed my Kindle and downloaded it, intent on scanning the whole thing, just looking for outrageous instances where the author got only Barbara's side of the story. I stood ready to cry "foul!"

Well, first of all, I had to stop speed-reading because the prologue on the book was so damn fascinating. I sat in my recliner, Windsor on my lap, an adult beverage nearby, and soaked up the historic story of the founding of *The Ladder*, the first lesbian publication to be distributed nationwide. It carried me away from there.

Also, early on it was pretty clear that the book's author was a crackerjack historian, working from original sources, personal correspondence, a phenomenal amount of research, and interviews with dozens, maybe hundreds of people. Even me. She'd interviewed me so long ago I'd forgotten she was doing the book. I remembered the call and our correspondence when a document I had given to her was referenced in a footnote. Cool.

So I devoured the book. It turned out to be an exquisitely researched biography and great read. It's an important look at the rise of lesbian publishing and a marvelous resource for preserving our history and culture—something you know I am passionate about.

And I was thrilled that when it came to the founding of Naiad, the book got it exactly right. In fact, even the criticisms about Anyda were true. I have to admit, she was imperious, classist, and a little bit haughty. Were her books literary masterpieces? No. But Anyda had the courage to write lesbian romance books and then fight like hell to see them published. Women all over the country adored her books because for the first time they could read about themselves in lesbian love stories with happy endings.

And Anyda, too, could be wonderfully generous, warm to her friends and fiercely determined to see a lesbian publishing house rise and thrive.

Were Anyda and Muriel silent partners in Naiad? Absolutely not. Their start-up funds and single-minded determination to find printers that would print lesbian books got the company started and kept it growing. But Anyda and Muriel aged and, yes, for the last 9 years of the partnership they were less and less involved in day-to-day operations.

All that being said, I did have two small corrections for a second edition. It was stated that Naiad Press had to pay to have Anyda's manuscripts typed. Not true, as Muriel did that for every single book. I saw the boxes and boxes of carbon copies.

Secondly, Anyda wrote a total of 14 books, not 13. The last one, *O'Mistress Mine* was published, by A&M Books, in 2003. I wish you could have seen a giddy 92-year-old pulling a book from a just-delivered carton and grinning as she waved it over her head.

And I would have liked to see one addition.

In one of the more memorable lesbian publishing scandals, Naiad Press published the book *Lesbian Nuns: Breaking Silence* in 1993. The book itself was an anthology of convent stories told by former nuns—quite wonderful and only scandalous to those who never expected to see the words *lesbians* and *nuns* in the same sentence.

Barbara Grier and Anyda were excited about the anthology because Barbara had been looking for a "crossover book," to bring lots of visibility to lesbian publishing. They knew this title could do the trick.

And did it ever!

There was a media explosion followed by national talk show interviews with the women who edited the anthology. Next came huge sales and the rare placement of a lesbian book in mainstream bookstore chains. Naiad's bet had paid off. Their financial future was given a huge boost and Naiad Press was the talk of the town.

However, scandal soon erupted.

Barbara Grier, working to maximize income for Naiad, offered excerpts from the books to gay and women's publications like *Philadelphia Gay News, Ms. Magazine* and *Christopher Street.* She also offered excerpts to *Forum Magazine*—a men's soft-core porn magazine published by *Penthouse.*

Holy cow. When Anyda found out about the *Forum Magazine* deal she was livid. A fierce feminist, she was practically apoplectic. Still very much involved in the business then, Anyda fumed to Barbara about the outrageous deal. She was disgusted at the betrayal of the women who wrote the essays, and embarrassed to see a Naiad excerpt in a "dirty magazine." She was still spouting off about it to me 15 years later.

The deal with *Forum* caused a huge stir in the lesbian literary community, and lots of folks were quoted about the scandal in *Indomitable*, but not Anyda.

After I finished reading the book, I wrote a gushing fan letter to author Joanne Passet, praising her research and the job she did, but asking only that one question: Why was Anyda not quoted regarding the *Lesbian Nuns: Breaking Silence* scandal?

Joanne wrote back to me, noting she'd thought she'd included Anyda's comments but it might have been deleted in editing. She did let me know that her research showed that Anyda tried to present a united front for Naiad during the scandal, and did not speak out publically even though she disagreed with Barbara's actions—also that Anyda's disappointment grew over time.

I can see that. But let me tell you, I got to hear a *lot* of Anyda's comments on the scandal over Dewar's Scotch and cheese and crackers while sitting on Anyda and Muriel's porch.

Face it. This was quite a story.

And you should read about it. All of it. *Indomitable: The Life of Barbara Grier* is a terrific book about our publishing, social and political history.

Read it now, because I have a feeling we need to remember our past as we confront our future. We need to be inspired by the pioneers who brought us so far. We need to be energized to get our butts back out on the streets with our placards and our bullhorns and our solidarity. A new political administration has been installed, and there are new threats against the gay rights we have fought so hard to win.

I intend to be at the Women's March on D.C., on the day after Inauguration Day, January 21, 2017. You may hear from me if I need bail money.

In the meantime, we have to stay indomitable. I love the book *Indomitable* and I am tickled that in the endnotes I am literally a footnote to history.

ACKNOWLEDGMENTS

Thanks first and always to my wife Bonnie, who, for some reason thought "we" were retiring. Instead she keeps me in stories as my partner in crime and hits the fairways while I slave over a hot computer. It's been a remarkable few years, in turns both scary and jubilant. So glad you are well, putting and puttering.

Thanks to Bywater Books for taking the leap to reissue my four previous collections and for publishing my latest screeds and antics.

To my Bywater mentors: Marianne K. Martin and Kelly Smith, you've been nonstop encouraging me since we first met in that over-landscaped, humid New Orleans courtyard more than a decade ago—cheering me on even as I was nominally a publishing "competitor." I'm proud to have you as my friends, editors and bosses. I'm even prouder I taught Kelly to drink cosmopolitans.

To my Bywater co-conspirators: Salem West, I've adored you since you offered, in print, to be my cabaña girl here at the beach. You're a treasure, personally and professionally—and besides, you introduced me to Ann McMan, delightful friend and genius cover designer. Good times ahead!

And a huge thank you to the magazine publishers/editors who keep me in ink—Steve Elkins and Murray Archibald (I love you both dearly), of *Letters from CAMP Rehoboth*, and to Terry Plowman of *Delaware Beach Life Magazine*. Your deadlines encourage me to go out and have crazy adventures, and I cannot thank you enough for the incentive—and the honor of being part of both of these remarkable publications.

Cheers to my chosen son Eric for the belly laughs and support—and for being an awesome blogger himself, alerting me to pop culture trends and unconscious bias. Love you.

And, once again, a very special nod to my BFF Stefani Deoul for trolling the Internet for bizarre stories to launch my essays, and being editor, accomplice, cheerleader, critic, therapist, and all the other things a friend really needs.

Never was the phrase "we get by with a little help from our friends" more fitting than the past few years for Bonnie and me. Thanks to Eloise for being there for us always; and to Nancy Hewish for being the stunt Bonnie, running sound and accompanying me on gigs when my wife was home recuperating. And thanks to all our friends who came along on adventures, when we were in sickness and in health, so we got through it all and I had something to write about.

Enormous hugs.

ABOUT THE AUTHOR

Fay Jacobs, a native New Yorker, spent 30 years in the Washington, D.C. area working in journalism, theatre and public relations. She's a humorist, storyteller and LGBT activist.

Her first book, *As I Lay Frying—a Rehoboth Beach Memoir* was published in 2004 and is in its fifth printing. Since then she has published *Fried & True—Tales from Rehoboth, For Frying Out Loud—Rehoboth Beach Diaries*, and *Time Fries—Aging Gracelessly in Rehoboth Beach.*

She has contributed feature stories and columns to such publications as *The Washington Post, The Advocate, OutTraveler, Curve Magazine, The Baltimore Sun, Chesapeake Bay Magazine, The Washington Blade, The Wilmington News Journal*, and more.

Since 1995 she has been a regular columnist for *Letters from CAMP Rehoboth*, and since 2010 she has had a monthly column in the award-winning *Delaware Beach Life Magazine.*

Since 2015, Fay has been touring with her one-woman show, *Aging Gracelessly: 50 Shades of Fay.*

She and Bonnie, her partner of 35 years and wife of five years, are aging in place in Rehoboth Beach, Delaware, with their spoiled schnauzer, Windsor. Fay is thrilled to have found a home at Bywater Books.

At Bywater Books we love good books about lesbians just like you do, and we're committed to bringing the best of contemporary lesbian writing to our avid readers. Our editorial team is dedicated to finding and developing outstanding writers who create books you won't want to put down.

We sponsor the Bywater Prize for Fiction to help with this quest. Each prizewinner receives $1,000 and publication of their novel. We have already discovered amazing writers like Jill Malone, Sally Bellerose, and Hilary Sloin through the Bywater Prize. Which exciting new writer will we find next?

For more information about Bywater Books and the annual Bywater Prize for Fiction, please visit our website.

www.bywaterbooks.com